SECRETS KEEP
YOU SICK

YOU ARE NOT YOUR MISTAKES

By Leslie Brennan

Daniel Gomez Enterprises, L.L.C.

Secrets Keep You Sick
You Are Not Your Mistakes
Written by Leslie Brennan

Published by Daniel Gomez Enterprises LLC /June 2025
Contact Info: (210) 663-5954 / Email: Info@DanielGomezGlobal.com

ISBN: 979-8-9991132-0-7

Dedication

This book is dedicated to the 11-year-old version of me—
The girl who carried too much, stayed quiet too often, and believed
she had to earn love to deserve it.
Sweet girl, you are loved. You are valuable. You are enough.
And I am so incredibly proud of you.

To my husband and children—
Thank you for walking this journey with me so faithfully. Even in the
storms, your steady love has been the anchor I didn't always know I
needed. You are my reason, my strength, and my joy.

To my 13 beautiful grandchildren—
You are the legacy I never dreamed I would have. Each of you
carries a piece of my heart and a story that's still being written. My
prayer is that you'll always walk in truth, grace, and the unwavering
knowledge that you are deeply loved. I pray this book leaves you a
blueprint of resilience, faith, and fierce love.
Never doubt your worth.

To the family and friends who stood in the gap—
Thank you for praying when I couldn't. For seeing light when I only
saw shadows. For showing grace, speaking truth, and sitting with
me in the hardest trenches.
You showed me what it means to be held—and to heal.
You know who you are,
and your love is woven into every page of this book.

Foreword

*"The spirit of a man can endure his sickness,
but as for a broken spirit, who can bear it?"*
—Proverbs 18:14 (NASB)

The process of therapy is, first and foremost, a sacred trust. The fact that an individual could find the strength within themselves to come and bare their soul before a stranger when everything in their world seems to be crashing in around them is nothing more than a sobering reminder that the place where we are standing is nothing short of sacred ground. As such, one must take extreme care that we, as therapists, create the space and place for them to bare their soul in safety.

To this author, the greatest offense of the therapist would be the violation of that trust in a manner that would result in the re-traumatization of the soul that is laid bare and naked before us in a place of incredible vulnerability. May it never be said of those who hold this trust that we would be so reckless with it in a manner that would invalidate their experience and bring further wounds to the wounded and broken spirit.

Secondly, therapy is a process, and as painful as it can be, one must learn to *"trust the process."* Yes, there are many claims by those who work in this field that a few sessions with a particular kind of therapy or technique, or a one-time prayer session with one individual, will result in instant change. However, more often than not, one will find that real and lasting change does not come easily, and it doesn't come instantly.

Pastor Chuck Swindoll once said in a sermon that *"instant change is as rare as it is phony."* No truer words have been spoken regarding real and lasting change. Long-held patterns developed over a lifetime, including strongholds over our lives, do not change overnight. Real and lasting change is a gradual process that requires great patience, grace, truth, and love. Prosci notes that *"change is not a one-time event, but rather an ongoing process of adaptation and improvement."* Once again, the therapist and the client must learn to trust the process."

Therapy is a place of validation. It is a validation of their experience, their story, their feelings, their emotions, their pain, their trauma, and their grief and loss. Too often, people have heard platitude after platitude from people who are more often than not uncomfortable with such experiences. The resulting thought of *"if this happened to them, this might happen to me"* is just too unsettling for others, but emotional honesty is essential for true healing to occur.

Repression, suppression, denial and the distortion of our experiences, feelings and emotions will only lead to further emotional, physical, psychological and spiritual damage Having said that, therapy is also a place of validation of the courage, the strength and the *"stick-to-it-iveness"* of the client who is willing to do the work that is necessary for real change to occur. Therapy is also a place for validating the changes we see in the client, giving them a word of encouragement when needed, validating things that need correcting, and challenging the client to continue even when their energy and willpower are spent. And make no mistake about it: therapy is real work, and if you are not doing the work and experiencing the full range of emotions and feelings that go with it, you are not doing therapy.

Therapy is a place of humility and surrender that involves letting go of our need to control every aspect of our lives. It is the realization that more often than not, our obsessive desire to control others and every aspect of our lives has gotten us where we are. Surrender thus becomes a voluntary act of submission and trust, whereby we relinquish control and embrace God's will and authority in our lives: *"not my will, but Thine."* For the therapist, humility often comes with the realization that *"there but by the grace of God, there go I."* With that comes the awareness that we are just humble guests and witnesses to a storyline that is already in progress and continues to be written, with or without us. Our clients lived before they became our clients, and their lives will continue and carry on as their storyline continues when they leave our office.

Thus, therapy also becomes a place of joy and celebration as we witness the power of change in the life of the individual sitting before us. To bear witness to the change that takes place in an individual is truly a humbling experience and a celebratory experience as well. As therapists, we want our clients not to need us, to go out and celebrate their experiences, and to embrace all that life has for them. Truly, *"weeping may endure for a night, but joy comes in the morning!"* There is no greater joy than to sit silently in your office as the client leaves and to celebrate with that, *"Yes, this is why I am here, this is why I do therapy: that others might truly live and experience the 'exceedingly, abundantly, above all that they could ever ask for or imagine!'"*

As a reader of this book, I invite you into a story that has been written, and is continuing to be written, by a client who has truly experienced the full range of emotions that therapy elicits. Note, also, that the author takes full ownership of the truth that this is their story. From apprehension, to pain, to burdens beyond one's ability to bear, to vulnerability, to the burdens of trauma—abuse, self-doubts, fear, loathing, to anger, abandonment, isolation, words that wound and not heal—experienced from help sought when there seemed to be no place else to go.

Bear witness to the courage and determination it takes to step out in faith again and seek the help she so desperately needed. You will bear witness to the truth spoken by Pastor Chuck Swindoll that *"instant change is as rare as it is phony!"* Bear witness to the work that therapy and change may demand from you, and ask yourself, *"Are you willing to pay the cost, and are you willing to do the work that therapy requires of you?"* Research on suicide across all countries, cultures, and people groups of the world reveals that the number one predictor of suicide is *"the absence of hope in the client's life."* Irvin Yalom states that the first task of the therapist is *"the creation of hope in the life of the client."*

"And thou shalt be secure, because there is hope; yea, thou shalt dig about thee and thou shalt take thy rest in safety" (Job 11:18, KJV).

Do you find yourself in a place where you are experiencing the absence of hope? Bear witness to the story of one who found a place of safety and did the digging necessary for change to occur and then experience the security that is found in the love, mercy, grace and compassion of the One who gave His all that we might not only have hope but also experience the freedom and security found in His love, mercy and grace.

- *Author Anonymous*

Table of Contents

Reflection & Renewal Tools

Introduction

It starts with an empty suitcase.
I leave mine until the very last moment.
I hate packing.

I hate trying to figure out what I'll feel comfortable wearing while I'm away, mostly because I've never been fully comfortable in my own skin. I pack, unpack, and repack, wrestling with how each outfit might make me feel. It may seem silly, but each one seems to carry the weight of how I imagine others will see me.

For as long as I can remember, I've struggled with a negative self-image and identity issues.

The truth is, the things inside my suitcase have never been simply the clothes.

There are also lies.
Shame.
Hurt.
Fear.

When we're born, we're handed a suitcase—not a physical one, but a life suitcase. It's filled, piece by piece, with the words spoken over us, the memories made around us, the beliefs shaped within us. Inside are the things that form us: joy and trauma, truth and confusion, comfort and chaos. As we grow, patterns settle in. Habits take hold. Stories begin to shape our reality.

We're lucky if we learn to occasionally unpack our suitcase and make space for healing and truth, but oftentimes, it gets shoved into a corner, too overwhelming to sort through. Then we pick up a new suitcase, and the cycle repeats.

This book is my journey.

It's the process of unpacking my life suitcase—completely.

Of confronting the lies I believed.
Of peeling back shame and letting grace in.
Of learning to forgive myself and others.
Of discovering the truth about who I am.
Of reclaiming my voice.
Of healing.

It's the story of how I learned to stop striving to be "*enough*"—and finally accepted that I already am. It's about learning to walk as a daughter of the King, living boldly, and trusting the God who never leaves—even in the silence.

As I began to unpack everything that was packed into me, I realized that, all along, I had been packing suitcases too.

As a mother, I hoped to fill my children's suitcases with strength, identity, purpose, and truth. I prayed over their futures and spoke life over their hearts. I tried to model love in action. I wanted them to know who they are and Whose they are—to grow up grounded in faith, resilient in hope, and rooted in kindness, courage, and character.

I hoped not to pack into them what I had to fight to unpack in myself.

And that is the heart of this book.

A story of unpacking.
A story of grace.
A story of becoming.

A Personal Note to the Reader

Before we go any further, I want to share something from my heart.

This book is not written to accuse or assign blame. These pages are filled with my personal experiences, reflections, and feelings. They are mine—just as your thoughts, emotions, and lived experiences are yours.

You are entitled to them. Full stop.

There are no ifs, ands, or buts. You have the right to feel what you feel—without apology, explanation, or permission.

I've come to understand that the wounds we carry are not always the result of one explosive moment or a single cruel word. Often, it's not the shout, but the whisper. Not the blow, but the pattern.

Just like one drop of water doesn't carve a canyon — but thousands of drops over time can wear through even the strongest stone — so too can repeated words, actions, or moments of neglect slowly shape how we see ourselves. A single instance might not leave a scar, but the steady drip of criticism, comparison, silence, or rejection can alter our self-worth, our voice, and our beliefs.

Sometimes it's not what was said to us, but what was left unsaid. Not what was done, but what was never undone.
Not the loud trauma — but the quiet erosion that took place over time.

> *"Our brains are shaped by repeated experience,*
> *not singular events."* — Dr. Bruce Perry

But here's what I've learned: those imprints do not have to define you forever, and while they may not have been your fault, the healing is still your responsibility. That's where growth begins.

I've also come to recognize that people don't always realize the way their words, actions, or silence will fall. They may not have intended harm. Many times, hurting people hurt people, and life's stressors can trigger reactions that are out of character, unfiltered, or unkind. That doesn't excuse the impact, but it helps to explain the pattern, and understanding opens the door to grace.

This book is not about blaming others.
It's about being brave enough to face the truth—and choosing what to do with it.

It's about growth.
It's about ownership.
It's about choosing to show up differently—for ourselves, and the generations coming after us.

Because here's the truth: life happens.
There is no magic fix. No easy button. No instant solution.
Good, bad, and messy—life shows up every single day.

And it's okay to sit with your emotions. To feel them. To name them. To honor them.
But we don't have to unpack and build our lives there.

"Feel it. Own it. But don't live there."

Eventually, we face a choice:
- Stay stuck in the story that broke us

or

- Step into the story we're being called to write next.

You can stay bitter—or you can get better.
You can replay the pain—or you can begin the healing.
You can stay seated in the dark—or you can rise into the light.

> *"Forgiveness is not saying the other person was right.*
> *It's saying you're choosing freedom over holding onto pain."*
> — Lysa TerKeurst

I chose growth. I chose grace. And I chose to believe that I am not the sum of what happened to me—I am the result of what God can do with me, through me, and despite it all.

And I hope, as you turn these pages, you'll feel empowered to do the same—at your own pace, and in your own time.

*This book may not reflect the perspective of all individuals involved and is based on the author's subjective recollection.

Chapter 1

Finding Grace

I'm not quite sure how grace got packed into my life suitcase. Or maybe, to be honest, sometimes I feel like it never was. Not for me, anyway. I saw grace given to others. I saw how others were forgiven, comforted, and celebrated despite their faults. But me? I never felt like I measured up. I tried everything I could to fit in—to be noticed, to matter. I told lies to protect myself. I hid secrets. I carried shame and guilt like armor, hoping it would somehow make me invisible and invincible at the same time. More than anything, I wanted what I did to be recognized for what it truly was— imperfect, yes, but sincere—not always perfect, but not always wrong either. I wanted to stop being haunted by what I should have done, said, or felt differently.

Grace always seemed reserved for others—the strong, the worthy, the already put-together. But also, somehow, for the weak, the quiet, the overlooked, the ones who seemed to have some unspoken pass. Everyone else fits somewhere in the circle of grace—everyone but me. I could speak about it. I could believe in it for everyone else, but not for myself.

I had faith. I believed the Scripture that said Jesus would leave the ninety-nine to find the one. I truly believed that if I were the only person alive, He would still come looking for me. I believed that I was the one He came for, but I still couldn't believe I deserved that kind of love and forgiveness. I was never mad at God. If anything, I believed that whatever good or bad happened to me, I must have deserved it. Somehow, it always felt like it was my fault. Grace was real, but I thought it was for the good people, the perfect people, the healed hearts, the ones who didn't carry so much mess. I knew God's love was unconditional, but somehow, I kept disqualifying myself from receiving it fully.

That realization came into sharp focus as I sat at a long table at the Wellspring Living Conference in Georgia. The woman leading the session unrolled a large spool of white paper, slicing off sections and placing them in front of the fifteen women seated with me. Another woman began drawing colored squares on a large whiteboard, labeling them with words: *marriage, birth, death, divorce, rape, incest, addiction, abortion, betrayal, hope, healing*.

The top of the board read: *"Family Tree"*.

The task was to create a tree on the blank paper and color-code the branches with the corresponding life events that had touched us. Some were branches of beauty. Some were branches of heartbreak. Some held both.

I sat frozen, staring at the paper. My throat tightened. I had never been in a room with strangers and been asked to identify, let alone publicly acknowledge, what felt like the deepest stains and scars of my life, and then that of my family lineage. It was like someone had handed me a mirror and said, *"Now trace the story."*

Just as I began to panic, the woman with the paper roll began to pray. She invited us to look at our story—no matter how broken, jagged, or incomplete—through the lens of grace.

That moment cracked something open in me.

You see, I've lived a life haunted by comparison. I've lived under the weight of not being enough. Not the smallest, not the smartest, not the prettiest, not the most loved. I wasn't the one people noticed. My voice was often dismissed, my feelings invalidated. I was told things didn't happen the way I had remembered. I was told I had misunderstood or overreacted.

The result? I began to believe that I was too much—and never enough—all at the same time.

Imposter syndrome became my constant companion—in motherhood, in ministry, in my work, and in my friendships. I was always second-guessing, always bracing for the moment someone would point out my flaws and say, "*See? I knew she wasn't good enough.*" So, I smiled. I performed. I succeeded. And I kept my wounds hidden behind a carefully curated version of strength.

I bought the lie that I didn't deserve good things. If I was blessed, it was by accident or pity or because someone hadn't figured out who I really was. When I messed up, I was ruthless with myself. Grace was a luxury I thought I couldn't afford.

But healing began with a whisper: What if grace is really for you, too?

💔 When Grace Feels Out of Reach

Here's the hard truth: Grace is hardest to accept when the voices around you constantly drag your past into the present.

It's hard to believe you've been made new when others continue to remind you who you used to be. When jokes are always at your expense. When people talk about you instead of to you. When you're the cautionary tale, not the redemption story. When forgiveness is preached but not practiced. That kind of commentary doesn't just sting—it digs trenches in your heart.

Psychologists refer to this as external shame reinforcement—when others' repeated reminders of your mistakes or failures shape your self-perception. According to Dr. Kristin Neff, a pioneer in self-compassion research, this repeated criticism from others can lead to increased self-judgment, decreased emotional resilience, and greater anxiety or depression.

And let's be honest—it's even harder when it comes from people who claim to love you. A snide comment at a family gathering. A sarcastic jab in a group chat. A *"prayer request"* laced with gossip. These things create internal scripts that whisper: *"You'll never outlive who you were. You'll always be 'that girl.'"* You are having your worst day.

But that's not what God says.

"Therefore, if anyone is in Christ, the new creation has come: The old has gone, the new is here!" — 2 Corinthians 5:17 (NIV)

Let me give you an example. I once overheard someone say, *"Well, you know how she is,"* with a chuckle. They didn't say it to my face. They didn't have the full story. But that comment found its way into my soul and nested there. I was back in middle school again—blamed for something I didn't do, feeling small, feeling like no matter how much I healed or grew, I would always be seen through a broken lens.

That moment reminded me that grace isn't just about forgiving others—it's about learning to walk in freedom even when others haven't forgiven you. It's about receiving what God says is true, even if the people around you still want to keep score.

Grace says, *"That version of me is gone. I'm not her anymore. And even if you can't see it yet—God does."*

So, if you've ever struggled to find grace because others won't let you forget who you were, I see you. More importantly, God sees you. Keep walking. Keep healing. Keep allowing Him to write your new story—even if the crowd around you continues quoting your old lines.

Confidence Over Comparison

They say, Be confident at all times.

But how do you do that when your inner monologue is on repeat with lies? When you've been shaped by silence or shadowed by shame? When everything inside you says you are not enough.

Healing begins when we stop measuring ourselves against someone else's highlight reel and begin listening to the truth of who God says we are.

Confidence is not about having it all together—it's about knowing you are deeply loved even in the undone places.

Love Yourself

It starts with forgiving yourself.

One of the most powerful tools in my journey was a book called *Scandalous Grace* by Julie Ann Barnhill. The first time I read it, I felt like she had stepped into my heart and voiced the exact words I hadn't been able to articulate. I've read it over and over again.

In Chapter 2, she shares a story about her grandmother baking homemade angel food cake. She describes the process in vivid detail—separating thirteen egg whites, the slow and careful whipping of ingredients, the quiet patience required, the beautiful rise of the cake in the oven. What struck me most, though, was the way she talked about the frosting.

Julie writes about how her grandmother would use two whole bricks of Philadelphia cream cheese, butter, vanilla, powdered sugar, and cream. And then, with unapologetic generosity, she would spread it, plop by plop, lavishly across the cake. No skimpy swipes. No holding back. She describes it as an exquisite exclamation point of confectionary grace.

And she ties that image to Jesus.

The grace He gives isn't measured or rationed. It's lavish. Audacious. Undeserved and overflowing.

I wept when I read that chapter. I could see my own grandmother in my mind's eye, baking two angel food cakes for my baby shower. I was 18, unmarried, and pregnant. I carried shame like it was stitched to my skin. I still remember the words spoken to me during that time—words that cut deep, words that wrote lies into my soul.

But I also remember her smile. Her gentle hands. Her love.

She looked at me and said, *"It doesn't matter how you got here. What matters is that you are here—and God has something special planned for you and this baby. You're not alone."*

I watched her cut strawberries and mix icing. I watched her love me when I couldn't love myself.

And I began to wonder, *"Could this kind of grace—the icing on the cake kind of grace—really be for me too?"*

The lady at the board's next words hit me just as deeply—right there in that conference dining room:

"May I just say something and get it out into the open? We are ALL dysfunctional. There isn't one of us who hasn't functioned abnormally at some point in time. There isn't one of us who has skated through life without an impairment of some sort tagging behind her."

Yes.

Yes, I needed to hear that.

Because I needed grace.

Not the filtered, pretty kind, but the real kind. The kind that meets you in the mess. The kind of grace that heals years of silence and shame. The kind that sets you free.

The lavish kind.

The kind that plops, spreads, and covers everything with the love of a Savior who never stopped pursuing me.

And I'm learning—slowly but surely—that grace is not just for everyone else.

It's for me, too.

But healing doesn't always come easily. Sometimes, we unknowingly perpetuate our pain. We find ourselves walking into the same types of relationships, situations, and cycles—reliving what hurt us, because we've grown comfortable in the chaos. Patterns form, and before we know it, they become our normal. We repeat what's familiar—even if it's damaging—because it's what we know. Hurting and broken people hurt and break other people.

The words that rang loudest in my ears weren't always meant to harm me, but over time, their weight compounded—shaping a narrative I began to believe about myself. Words spoken, whispered, or even muttered in passing started to write the script in my mind.

The enemy of our lives thrives on that script. He desires that we believe the lies—every single one of them. The ones hurled at us. The ones we speak to ourselves. The ones we let echo louder than the truth.

But the truth is louder—when we're finally ready to listen.

Grace truly found me at the very end of myself, in the middle of 2022. I was unraveling. I didn't know how much more I could carry. I was tired, discouraged, and done trying to hold it all together. A friend recommended a Christian therapist—and one day, when I couldn't take another comment, another situation, another thought or breath under the weight of it all—I called. And that call changed everything.

Grace came to me not in a sermon or a book that day, but in a conversation. It came in the form of someone saying, *"It's okay to feel exactly what you're feeling."* For the first time in my life, I felt truly heard. No one was listening to correct me, shame me, invalidate my experiences, or later use my words as weapons. No. This was different.

This was grace—sitting with me in the muck and the mire, in the tears and suffocating emotions, and simply acknowledging, *"This sucks, and it's okay to say it."*

That Christian therapist I called back in 2022? He's still walking this journey with me. We meet weekly—even now, as I write this book. He's helped me begin the hard work of unpacking my suitcase piece by piece. Some of those pieces are heavy. Some are tangled in pain and confusion. Some, he and I both know, still need time—and grace—to face. He gives me that space. In my time. In God's time.

He reminds me often that he's proud of me. Not just for surviving, but for doing the work. For showing up. For telling the truth. He's taught me more than I can ever fully express about what it means to hold space—to be present, to listen, to witness pain without fixing it or rushing it away.

There are areas of my life that I've asked God to pour out grace and forgiveness, and where unpacking would only cause more harm. Places where He has gently covered what I wasn't ready to face. He has begun the cleansing work that only He can do. Healing doesn't always mean full exposure. Sometimes healing is letting God handle what I don't yet have the strength to touch.

And even there—especially there—grace still shows up.

And somewhere in the middle of that mess, I found my Mary.

Now, my Mary may not be like your Mary. My Mary came into my life during a devastating time and never once asked me to be anything other than exactly who I was. She was the kind of friend who would have committed a crime with me just to let me know I wasn't alone. (No felonies or misdemeanors were committed, for the record.) She taught me that when I say I'm *"F.I.N.E."*

(Frustrated. Insecure. Neurotic. Emotional.), she's down to ride it out with me. She embodied grace, and through her, I began to believe in the possibility of grace for me, too.

For a long time, I believed love had to be earned.
That friendship had to be proven.
That affirmation had to be chased.

I thought my place in someone's life depended on how well I performed. I worked hard to be lovable, to be needed, and to be noticed. I thought if I could just be enough, I would finally be worthy.

But grace doesn't play by those rules.

Grace isn't transactional. It isn't measured out based on merit or appearance, or perfection. Grace says you are already enough—not because of what you've done, but because of who you are and Whose you are.

When you've lived in survival mode, grace feels unnatural. It's not earned. It's freely given. And for someone like me, that felt impossible to accept. Because I'd been shaped by experiences that told me I had to earn love. I had to prove my value. I had to hold everything together or risk being left behind.

But grace doesn't require performance. Grace says you belong— right here and right now, even in this.

The enemy of our lives thrives when we believe love is conditional. He whispers lies that love must be earned, that we are too much or never enough. He twists the truth until we carry shame in silence, convinced that even God's grace has limits.

But grace breaks the cycle. Grace unpacks the lie. Grace sits in the mess with you and gently reminds you—you are not beyond repair. You are not too broken to be made whole.

Grace restores.
Grace holds space.
Grace stays.

And maybe, just maybe, we were never meant to earn love at all.

We were simply meant to receive it.

📖 Reflection & Renewal: Journal and Action Steps

📜 Scriptures for Meditation:

- **2 Corinthians 12:9** – "But He said to me, 'My grace is sufficient for you, for my power is made perfect in weakness.' Therefore, I will boast all the more gladly about my weaknesses, so that Christ's power may rest on me."

- **John 1:16** – "For from His fullness we have all received, grace upon grace."

- **Hebrews 4:16** – "Let us then approach God's throne of grace with confidence, so that we may receive mercy and find grace to help us in our time of need."

- **Psalm 103:8** – "The Lord is compassionate and gracious, slow to anger, abounding in love."

- **1 Peter 5:10** – "And the God of all grace, who called you to His eternal glory in Christ, after you have suffered a little while, will Himself restore you and make you strong, firm and steadfast."

Journal Prompts:

1. Where in your life have you been striving to earn love, affirmation, or belonging?

2. What lies have you believed about your worth, and where did they originate?

3. Can you identify any patterns or behaviors that kept you performing for love rather than receiving it?

4. What would it look like for you to accept grace without conditions?

5. Who are the people in your life who have shown you grace, and how did their love impact your healing?

✅ Next Steps to Walk Out Healing

1. Choose one scripture from this list and reflect on it daily for a week.

2. Begin naming the lies you've believed and replacing each one with a truth from God's Word.

3. Practice receiving without performing—say "*yes*" to rest, help, or kindness without guilt.

4. Share your story with someone safe, or begin writing it down to explore your journey honestly.

You're not just reading a chapter—you're living a breakthrough. Keep going. God's not done with your story. Not even close.

📑 Acknowledgments, Citations & Further Reading:

Portions of this chapter were inspired by or reference insights from:

- Julie Ann Barnhill, *Scandalous Grace*

- *Theophostic Prayer Ministry* concepts from Dr. Ed Smith

- *Life Review Therapy*, APA Dictionary of Psychology

- Christian counseling practices related to narrative healing and grace-based recovery

- Neff, K. (2003). *Self-Compassion: An Alternative Conceptualization of a Healthy Attitude* Toward Oneself. *Self and Identity*, 2(2), 85–101.

Chapter 2

See Myself as He Sees Me

Unpacking the things I carried in my suitcase—layer after painful layer—led me to one of the hardest and most beautiful revelations of my life: learning to see myself as He sees me.

And let me say this up front: this is still a daily process. At the time of writing this book, I still find myself taking my thoughts captive every single day. I still have to intentionally interrupt the old scripts that want to replay in my mind and choose to do something different. It's a conscious decision every day to exchange old defaults for God's truth. This journey doesn't get easier overnight—it gets deeper. More anchored. More intimate. And grace meets me there each time I return.

I didn't arrive here easily—and by *"arrive,"* I mean getting to the place where:

- I realized I needed a new lens through which to view myself.
- I figured out I had to silence the noise, the voices, and begin rewriting the script in my mind.
- I came to understand that how He sees me is completely different than how I see myself.

- Accepting that this process might just be a rinse-and-repeat kind of thing—sometimes day by day, sometimes minute by minute—until it rewrites the narrative of my days, resets my thoughts, and renews my mind.

It wasn't some overnight transformation. It was slow. Gentle. Gritty. And full of grace. Sometimes, it takes hearing the same truth over and over in different ways before it sinks in. Before the "*ah-ha*" moment finally breaks through the noise and I realize—Hello, Leslie... He is speaking to YOU.

God had been whispering it all along. Through people. Through prayer. Through truth. But I was so caught up in my own noise and shame, I couldn't recognize it. But grace has a way of repeating itself. Of circling back. Of making sure we don't miss it—especially when we're the ones who need it most.

So, before I ever started seeing myself differently, I first had to believe that His voice was actually speaking to me.

As I began to unpack some of the dark moments in my story and examine where God was in the midst, I was filled with anxiety. Though there were things done to me without my consent, there were also times in my life when I felt that what others needed or wanted from me was for their benefit—and if that left me feeling empty and shamed, well, that was just the price to pay.

I had a reel that played in my mind like an old, clunky reel-to-reel projector. No sound—just images. Cracked, hazy, and choppy. Sections of my story I would have done anything to take back, not remember, and erase. Things I begged God to remove from my thoughts. Moments that were packed with so much shame and remorse.

Let me stop and tell you where I fell apart.

I unraveled in 2022 after a series of events, many of which I'll unpack later in this book. What matters for now: I had no control over my circumstances. These weren't consequences of my own mistakes. These were waves that came crashing in without warning, without mercy.

And still, I blamed myself.

The noise in my head was deafening. It wasn't just loud—it was paralyzing. Every breath felt like a war. I was exhausted from trying to keep it together, to stay strong, and to smile through pain I didn't know how to name. I was unraveling—not just emotionally, but spiritually, mentally, and physically. I didn't see a way forward. The weight of everything was pressing in on all sides, and the thoughts I'd spent years trying to silence came back louder than ever.

I didn't want to keep going—not like that. I couldn't.

And yet... it was in that place—utterly undone, out of answers, drowning in the noise—that God showed Himself faithful. He didn't wait for me to get it together. He met me at rock bottom. Not to scold me or to lecture me—but to hold me. To remind me that His grace doesn't expire just because I'm tired of trying.

It was in those moments that He began to unpeel the layers and unpack the junk. He shifted it to the top of my suitcase, as if to say, *"We must address this issue and deal with it, once and for all."* Healing, I've learned, is a lot like peeling an onion. One layer comes off, and you think you're done—then life squeezes just a little, and the next layer rises to the surface. And sometimes, it stings. Sometimes, it brings tears. Sometimes, it's a layer you didn't even know was there. But every layer removed is a step closer to the heart of who you are—and to the truth of who God says you've always been.

I didn't realize, in those moments, that through all the wrong turns, the hurt, the heartache, the mistakes, the laughter, the smiles, the memories, and the tears, He was actually working all things together for His glory.

He was redeeming my story. I had internalized every shortcoming, every mistake, every reprimand, every failure, every cruel joke, every backhanded comment, every moment I was left out, overlooked, or told I was "*too much*" or "*not enough.*" When you're shaped by criticism instead of compassion, it carves cracks in your identity. Those cracks don't just stay put—they deepen into beliefs that say, "*You're unlovable, unworthy, unwanted.*"

Words spoken to me, and about me, and even words spoken to others, shaped the script inside my head. When another child is praised for being "*so sweet and tiny,*" while you're told to "*watch what you eat,*" those words don't just land—they echo. When you're made to exercise in front of others or scolded differently than your siblings, that will send messages. Loud ones. And the child inside begins to interpret those moments as, "*I'm the problem. I'm not okay the way I am.*"

Those messages don't just go away. They become the soil where shame takes root—and eventually, they blossom into behavior patterns, defense mechanisms, or hiding places.

So, when God began whispering a different truth, it took me time to believe it. But slowly, gently, faithfully—He rewrote it.

The event that led me to therapy was my husband's stroke. Life unraveled—there is no other way to express it. It was as if everything that had been held together by tape, glue, and pressure exploded into a thousand bits and pieces. The mental and emotional breakdowns, coupled with so many other losses, were finally winning.

As I sat, tears streaming, and made the decision in 2022 to finally call the therapist my friend had talked to me about, I was at the end. I had made such a mess of my life, and now life circumstances were making a new mess of my life. Of my husband's life. It was breaking him down and destroying his very fabric. Mine too.

I didn't realize that the breaking was the beginning of healing. Inside the pain, the purpose would be revealed.

I had just finished reading a book my therapist recommended— *God Never Gives Up on You* by Max Lucado.

The message hit me like a wave: *"God's grace is for the Strugglers Among Us and the Fumblers Within Us."* That was me—part saint, part scoundrel. I meant well, but I didn't always do well. I had breakthroughs and breakdowns—often in the same hour. I didn't need reminders of my failures; I wore them like labels. But I desperately needed to be reminded of God's unwavering grace.

Max wrote about Jacob—a man who wasn't the prodigy, but the prodigal. A man who was clever but lacked conscience. He deceived his brother, tricked his father, ran from conflict, and limped his way through much of life. And yet, God never gave up on him.

As I read those pages, I began to see a reflection of my own story in Jacob's. And for the first time, I started to believe—maybe God hadn't given up on me either. Maybe He saw me not as I saw myself, but as He created me to be.

Maybe, just maybe, I was still usable. Still valuable. Still wanted.

Not despite my wounds—but because of them.

Not because I had it all together—but because I finally let it fall apart in His presence.

I sat crying. Pouring out my heart to God—loudly—in my home office. Tears streaming, speaking out ugly truths as if He didn't already know. I asked Him to meet me here at the well and fill me. I begged Him to uproot whatever needed to be uprooted so I could finally, after over 50 years, become who He truly created me to be. I lay on my couch in the fetal position and crawled into the lap of God. I begged Him to hold me. And I wept. Sobbed. Gut-wrenching, cleansing, purifying tears. I didn't want to start and fail—I wanted to start, dig out, uproot, overhaul, and be new. Be whole. See myself like He does. Have a new default setting.

This kind of purifying had nothing to do with perfection—it had everything to do with surrender. I began to realize that purification often requires heat, pressure, and pain before it reveals beauty.

Precious metals like gold and silver are refined through intense heat—fire that melts away impurities and brings forth the pure element beneath. Similarly, gemstones are formed under incredible pressure and time, shaping them into objects of breathtaking beauty. The refining fire isn't meant to destroy; it's meant to define. (See: Zechariah 13:9, Isaiah 48:10, and 1 Peter 1:7.)

God was doing that with me.

He wasn't burning me down. He was burning off what didn't belong.

He wasn't crushing me to break me. He was shaping me under pressure into something strong, radiant, and whole.

This was purification that led to restoration. The kind that only comes when we fall apart in the right place—into the arms of grace.

I had no idea at that moment what was coming. I just knew I needed a real change—a lasting change. A healing. I didn't want to be in "*remission*" with a chance of this junk coming back up. I wanted to cut it away. I don't know how long I cried. How long I lay there.

I fell asleep and woke with peace and a clear direction. If I were going to begin to see myself as He sees me, I was going to have to take every single thought captive.

Later, I would realize—I had experienced my own *Woman at the Well* moment.

The story of the nameless Samaritan woman at the well, recorded only in the Gospel of John, is a revealing one, full of many truths and powerful lessons for us today. The story of the woman at the well follows on the heels of the account of Jesus' interaction with Nicodemus, a Pharisee and prominent member of the Jewish Sanhedrin (John 3:1–21). In John 4:4-42 we read about Jesus' conversation with a lone Samaritan woman who had come to get water from a well (known as Jacob's well) located about a half mile from the city of Sychar, in Samaria.

This was an extraordinary woman. She was a Samaritan—a race of people that the Jews utterly despised as having no claim on their God. She was an outcast and was looked down upon even by her own people. This is evidenced by the fact that she came alone to draw water from the community well when, during biblical times, drawing water and chatting at the well was the social high point of a woman's day. However, this woman was ostracized and marked as immoral—an unmarried woman living openly with the sixth in a series of men.

"The story of the woman at the well teaches us that God loves us despite our bankrupt lives. God values us enough to actively seek us, to welcome us to intimacy, and to rejoice in our worship. As a result of Jesus' conversation, only a person like the Samaritan woman—an outcast from her own people—could understand what this means. To be wanted and cared for when no one, not even herself, could see anything of value in her—this is grace indeed." (Source: GotQuestions.org)

Seeing myself as He sees me has been like peeling an onion. At first, I was only aware of the dry, crunchy outer layers—the protective coverings I had learned to wear. These were the things I let the world see: my performance, my put-togetherness, my smile, my silence. They were rough and brittle, and they weren't really me—but they kept me feeling safe.

As I began to trust God more deeply, I started peeling back those layers. And with every layer I removed, I found more pain underneath. Some layers were shameful. Some were fear. Others were bitterness, lies I believed, or words spoken over me. Each one had to be peeled back slowly, and sometimes painfully. Every time I peeled, there were tears.

Underneath all those layers—buried deep in the center—was the truth: the me He sees. The one He formed in my mother's womb. The one He knows by name. The one He calls beloved. That core, that center, was never ugly to Him. It was always beautiful. Worth saving. Worth redeeming.

Healing isn't always instant. It's layer by layer. Tear by tear. Grace by grace.

And through it all, God never stops seeing the whole me—even when I'm just starting to.

But seeing myself as He sees me wasn't just a spiritual revelation—it had to become a daily, intentional discipline. I had to change the people, places, and things influencing my thoughts, identity, and story. We'll dive deeper into this later, but I can't stress enough how vital it is to begin taking every thought captive. It's like prepping your meals before starting a diet—you need to do the work ahead of time, if you want sustainable results.

For me, that meant sitting down and taking a hard look at the people in my life and the roles they were playing. Who was in my circle? Who was speaking into the pages of my story? It's always good to have a sounding board. My Mary—she listened and listened. If my story called for a "*that jerk*!" moment, she let him have it. If it needed a laugh or a cry, she was my girl. If it required a harsh dose of reality and some sense knocked into me, she was there with sleeves rolled up and truth in hand—even when I didn't want to hear it. She, like my therapist, knew what I needed to learn.

God wants all the parts of the story. He wants to sit in the mess with us, no matter how dirty. He wants to give us our moment. He would prefer to go first, but He will wait—He will let us lead if that's what it takes to get us to where we can finally hear Him.

He is. He always has been. From the moment I was conceived, He's been waging war for me. He's fought for my life, my heart, my healing, and my purpose.

And let me say this—who you surround yourself with matters. Who is in your circle matters. It is hard to see the fingerprints of God on your story when you're in the wrong company. The same goes for the activities that fill your time. If you think what you watch, read, or listen to doesn't matter, I can assure you—it does.

Studies show that repeated exposure to negative media and social comparison significantly increases anxiety, depression, and distorted self-image (American Psychological Association, 2017). Content filled with fear, comparison, or toxicity has the power to shape your narrative before you even realize it.

But truth reshapes and truth sets free.

We'll come back to this, but for now, know this: grace has to be paired with intention, and intention has to be rooted in truth.

I had to begin changing my day. I had to build in time to grow spiritually again—time in prayer and devotion. Some people had certain positions in my life that God desired to shift. I had to let Him. I changed what I listened to in the car and at home. I began playing contemporary Christian music—songs with meaning and purpose that didn't take me back to a dark place or a painful memory.

Music has a way of doing that. Do you ever hear a song and suddenly you're 14 again, watching a memory play like a movie in your mind? That can be beautiful—but for me, those flashbacks often triggered chains of guilt, shame, worthlessness, and remorse. I had to eliminate that possibility by checking my media intake—not just music, but social media, apps, television, and more.

Garbage in, garbage out—right?

2023 began with a 21-day fast and a heartfelt invitation to God to start digging out the junk. Much of that *"junk"* was right here—in my mind. What was going in, was feeding the things I desperately wanted to starve, and it had to stop.

It was during that fast that I also gave up my wine. I love a good glass of red, especially paired with dark chocolate, but God spoke clearly to my heart—this wasn't just a harmless indulgence. It was a coping mechanism. A disguised escape. And while it looked like pleasure, it had roots in my past that would only continue to hurt me and delay the healing I longed for.

There were also places. Places I had to redefine my relationship with—sometimes because of the people who occupied them. I had to learn to set boundaries: When I would go. If I could go. How long would I stay? What I would allow myself to engage with while I was there.

Steve Arterburn, founder of New Life Ministries, said it best in his work on recovery: *"You can't heal in the same environment that made you sick."* He teaches that true transformation comes when we take bold action to change our people, places, and things—not because we're running, but because we're finally ready to be free.

And I was ready.

Steve Arterburn also teaches that boundaries are not walls of isolation but bridges to restoration. Setting them is not about shutting others out—it's about inviting God in to show us who truly belongs in the intimate spaces of our lives. We are reminded by his recovery teachings that healthy boundaries will protect progress and preserve peace. They allow us to live in grace without constantly being pulled back into cycles of guilt, shame, and confusion.

Changing your people, places, and things isn't selfish. It's sacred. It's brave. It's part of the healing.

When we begin to remove the things that bind us, we make room for the One who breaks every chain.

📖 Reflection & Renewal: Journal and Action Steps

📜 Scriptures for Meditation:

- **2 Corinthians 10:5** – "*We take captive every thought to make it obedient to Christ.*"

- **Romans 12:2** – "*Do not conform to the pattern of this world, but be transformed by the renewing of your mind.*"

- **Psalm 139:13–14** – "*For you created my inmost being; you knit me together in my mother's womb... I am fearfully and wonderfully made.*"

- **Zephaniah 3:17** – "*The Lord your God is with you, the Mighty Warrior who saves. He will take great delight in you... will rejoice over you with singing.*"

- **Zechariah 13:9** – "*I will bring that group through the fire and make them pure. I will refine them like silver and test them like gold.*"

Journal Prompts:

1. What thoughts or beliefs do you carry that don't align with how God sees you?

2. Can you remember a moment where you felt unworthy, but looking back, you now see God was present and working?

3. What are some "outer layers" you've been hiding behind? What would it look like to start peeling one back?

4. When was the last time you truly felt seen, heard, and held by God? What did that feel like?

1. What does it mean to you to "take every thought captive"? What's one practical way you can start doing this each day?

✅ Next Steps to Walk Out Healing

1. Surround yourself with people who speak life and truth.

2. Create a sacred space—through journaling, scripture, or prayer—where you can regularly unpack and reflect.

3. Identify one lie each day and actively replace it with scripture.

4. Speak a daily affirmation based on God's truth over yourself.

5. Track your thought life—note when you drift into old narratives, and gently redirect with truth.

You're not just reflecting—you're renewing. Keep peeling back the layers. Grace is doing a deeper work.

📖 Acknowledgments, Citations & Further Reading:

Portions of this chapter were inspired by or include references to:

- Max Lucado, *God Never Gives Up on You*

- GotQuestions.org, "The Woman at the Well" summary of John 4

- Steve Arterburn, *New Life Ministries*, teachings on recovery and boundaries

- *American Psychological Association* (2017), findings on media and mental health

For a complete list of resources and additional study materials, please refer to the Acknowledgments & Citations section at the back of this book.

Chapter 3
You Are Not Your Mistakes

Grace showed up in the mess—in the middle of the unraveling, when everything I had taped and glued together finally split wide open. I had spent years trying to hold it all together, believing that if I could perform well enough or serve long enough, maybe I could make up for the mess behind the curtain, but when grace came, it didn't ask for performance. It asked for surrender.

When grace came in, it required me to start removing those masks. It required me to look honestly at my authentic self—not who I thought I had to be to earn love or keep peace, but who I was underneath it all. That brought tears and pain, because when I finally saw myself clearly, I didn't feel strong, capable, or worthy. I felt like a failure. A mess. Anything but enough. Grace exposed what I was hiding—but it didn't come to shame me. It came to heal me.

We all make mistakes. No one's life is perfect. Every one of us has moments we wish we could do over—choices we'd change if we could. I've made mistakes that haunted me, some so heavy that there were many times I didn't care if I woke up the next morning. In those dark seasons, my children pulled me through—because they needed their mom.

It's important to unpack some of those mistakes here, even partially, because they became the root of many of the lies I believed about myself. I carried shame from sexual abuse I experienced both as a child and as a teen. I carried guilt from a failed marriage, and the weight of not being the kind of mother I thought I should have been—the kind who protected her children from every emotional wound or harmful influence. I carried shame from walking away from the Lord. I internalized every criticism as an attack and wore embarrassment like a second skin. I carried sin I don't want to pour out onto this page, because I've already poured it out before the throne of grace.

One of the deepest areas of shame came from the years I lived in confusion about love and my own worth. Like many survivors of childhood sexual abuse, I experienced something that researchers and counselors often describe as **"distorted attachment."** According to the National Child Traumatic Stress Network, early abuse can disrupt a child's understanding of boundaries, trust, and affection. Abuse teaches the lie that love and pain are linked—that approval must be earned through self-sacrifice, and that our bodies are objects rather than sacred.

For some survivors, this confusion can result in repeated patterns of exploitation or promiscuity—not out of rebellion, but because abuse taught them to associate affection with harm. As counselor and trauma expert Dr. Dan Allender writes, *"Children do not sin when they are sinned against, but the wounds they carry often become the source of great confusion and shame that leads to further wounding."* That was true for me. I didn't want those things. I didn't feel empowered. I felt empty. Part of me believed this was all I deserved—that this was somehow what love looked like.

When I did sin—when I made choices outside of God's will—it only added to the mountain of shame already crushing me. I didn't know how to separate what had been done to me from what I had chosen in response to it. I blamed myself for all of it. Because I believed I wasn't lovable without being needed or used, I became a magnet for relationships and environments that reinforced those false beliefs.

These mistakes didn't define me, but for years, I let them, and until I began untangling the roots of that shame, I couldn't receive grace. I couldn't see the love of God clearly. I thought I had to fix myself before He could fully love me, but grace came anyway and healing began—not all at once, but layer by layer.

The journey began with unpacking the suitcase I'd been dragging through life—shame, brokenness, lies about my worth. Then came the mirror: seeing myself through God's eyes, not through the distorted lens of my past. I began taking every thought captive and slowly peeling away the layers of self-protection I had worn for decades.

That's when I truly saw it—codependency. Not for the first time, but this time, I recognized it for what it really was. The roles I had played for so long—the fixer, the peacekeeper, the over-functioner—weren't just personality traits or helpful habits. They were masks. They were survival strategies, deeply rooted in a painful belief I had carried for years: that I was only as valuable as what I could do, fix, or manage. I began to understand that these roles weren't just responses to difficult circumstances—they were ways I tried to earn worth, ways to avoid confronting the quiet lie that I was nothing more than my failures and mistakes.

An **over-functioner** tends to take on more than their fair share of responsibility in relationships or situations—often stepping in to fix, manage, or control things for others, especially during stress or crises. They may do this to feel needed, secure, or in control, but it often comes at the expense of their own needs, emotions, or well-being.

Over-functioning is a behavioral pattern, often rooted in anxiety and learned survival responses, where a person compensates for others by doing more than is healthy or necessary—emotionally, mentally, or practically. Over-functioners tend to believe *"if I don't do it, it won't get done"* or *"everything depends on me."*
— Adapted from Dr. Harriet Lerner, *The Dance of Connection.*

Traits of an Over-Functioner:

- Takes charge in nearly every situation (even when not asked).
- Has trouble delegating or trusting others to follow through.
- Often exhausted but struggles to say no.
- Feels resentful but hides it under performance or perfectionism.
- Tries to fix other people's problems or emotions.
- Avoids vulnerability by staying *"strong"* or *"busy."*

Why It Matters:

Over-functioning is often used as a mask for deep-seated fears—fear of being unworthy, fear of failure, fear of being abandoned or rejected. It's a trauma response, especially for those who learned early on that love had to be earned through performance or service. It's a major player in codependent dynamics and can prevent true healing by keeping us from sitting with our own needs or allowing others to carry their own weight.

Well, there you have it. It comes as no surprise that my life suitcase was packed with codependency. Codependency—this wasn't my first introduction to it. It was something I knew I struggled with. It was one of the layers that needed to be completely removed. As I continued unpacking the layers of shame, fear, and survival in my life suitcase, one word began to surface more clearly—codependency was still present. The real work wasn't just admitting it—it was identifying why and how codependency had shown up and taken root in my life. It was understanding how that role shaped my identity, decisions, and relationships. It wasn't easy to face.

Codependency, for me, became a way of covering up the lie that I was my mistakes. If I could keep everyone else okay, maybe I could quiet the ache deep inside me. I thought if I could earn love, prove my worth, or avoid conflict, I could finally outrun the guilt and shame I carried, but the truth is, codependency doesn't heal the wound. It just buries it deeper under the weight of constant performance. I wasn't rescuing others. I was trying to redeem myself.

To better understand it, let me share how I've come to define codependency in my own life:

At its core, codependency is a misplaced identity. It's when your worth becomes wrapped up in someone else's well-being, approval, or acceptance. It's the belief—spoken or unspoken—that if I can just keep everyone else okay, then maybe I'll be okay too.

Clinically, it's been called *"relationship addiction."* It shows up as the need to save, fix, or please others at the expense of your own emotional health. You may be over-functioning, shrinking your needs, or walking on eggshells to maintain peace. You become so focused on another person's happiness or stability that you lose your own sense of self.

But for me, codependency wasn't just a behavior pattern. It was the echo of my unhealed pain. It was survival. It was the mask I wore to feel worthy—because deep down, I believed my value came from what I could do, not from who I was.
—Portions inspired by *HelpGuide.org's* definition of codependency.

That need to earn love or approval—especially through self-sacrifice—often led me into a pattern I now understand more clearly. When something I did made someone else happy, I clung to it like a lifeline. I thought, *"That's it. Do more of that. Then they'll like you. Then you'll matter. Then you'll be good enough."* Even if that behavior left me feeling ashamed, afraid, or disgusted with myself, it didn't matter because their happiness seemed more important than my peace. If you used me to get what you wanted, and it kept you needing me, then in my mind, it was worth it. It was a sick, sad tangle of lies.

Clinically, this type of thinking is often tied to what's called a trauma bond—a psychological response—where a person becomes attached to someone who is harming them, because of the intensity and unpredictability of the relationship. According to the National Domestic Violence Hotline, trauma bonding *"occurs when a person experiencing abuse develops an unhealthy attachment to the abuser."* In situations involving emotional manipulation, control, or codependency, the brain can begin to associate pain with love, and sacrifice with safety.

I wasn't just caught in unhealthy patterns—I was tangled in emotional survival, and somewhere deep inside, I began to realize that I didn't even truly understand what love was. I had confused being needed with being loved. Love, by definition, is not about control, obligation, or sacrifice at the cost of your soul. According to 1 Corinthians 13:4-7, love is patient, kind, not self-seeking, not easily angered, and keeps no record of wrongs. It always protects, always trusts, always hopes, and always perseveres. That kind of love doesn't manipulate or demand—it frees, heals, and reflects the heart of God.

Yet, so many of my ideas about love were formed from wounds instead of the Word. Love wasn't supposed to cost me my peace, but the version I had come to know did—and I accepted that version because I thought it was all I deserved.

It was around this time that my therapist asked me to try something simple, yet deeply uncomfortable: to create a personal timeline. Not just a list of milestones, but a reflective sequence of the events—good and bad—that shaped me. The moments that stood out when I pressed rewind on the tape of my life. In counseling, this exercise is often called a *"life review"* or a *"life timeline,"* a form of narrative therapy. According to the American Psychological Association, life review therapy is a guided process that helps people make sense of their past experiences and integrate them into a healthier self-identity.

What I discovered was both heartbreaking and healing. I could clearly see the patterns—when I started to perform for love, when I first felt invisible, when I began attaching my worth to someone else's approval. Some moments, I had buried deep, thinking I had moved on. Others I relived far too often without ever facing them, but putting it all on paper helped me to connect the dots. It helped me understand that I wasn't in my worst moments. And just because those things happened to me—or through me—didn't mean they were me. (Source: American Psychological Association; *Life Review Therapy, APA Dictionary of Psychology*.)

Alongside the timeline, my therapist led me through another vital process—something known in Christian counseling circles as "*The Healing Timeline*" or "*Life Mapping,*" a method often used in inner healing or Theophostic-style prayer ministry. It's a practice of not just naming events, but pausing at each point to ask, "*What lie did I come to believe in that moment? What was spoken over me? And where was God?*"

This isn't just about memory—it's about meaning. According to Christian counselor and author Dr. Mark Virkler, identifying these lies and replacing them with God's truth is core to healing the wounded places in our identity. It's where we learn to let Jesus step into those moments with us—not to erase them, but to redeem them.

That practice changed everything. I began to see that the lies I had internalized—about my worth, my guilt, my role—were never God's words, and when I invited Him into those moments, He didn't show up with condemnation. He showed up with compassion. (Source: Virkler, Mark. "*Prayers That Heal the Heart*." Communion With God Ministries, 2001.)

Some hard work was underway. Not just the hard work of silencing old lies, but also of identifying the words still being spoken by the people around me—words that were wounding me daily. My therapist once shared a quote by Mark Twain: "*It takes your enemy and your friend, working together, to hurt you to the heart; the one to slander you and the other to get the news to you. He gossips habitually; he lacks the common wisdom to keep still that deadly enemy of man, his own tongue.*"

This quote sheds light on the deeply wounding nature of gossip. It's one thing when enemies aim to harm you—but it's often the careless whispers of those you once trusted that cut the deepest. Gossip doesn't always roar with open hostility; sometimes it tiptoes in through a friend or family member's retelling, dressed as concern or curiosity. Whether spread with intention or shared without thought, the damage is real. Words, once released, can become weapons—shaping stories, staining reputations, and stirring pain long after the moment has passed. This is a powerful reminder to guard our tongues and our hearts, and to be people who protect rather than provoke.

This quote has stuck with me because it wasn't just the lies I believed about myself—it was the reinforcement of those lies by people I trusted. He told me I had permission to ask certain people to stop delivering those messages—messages of slander, gossip, or criticism disguised as concern. If someone hated or disliked me, I didn't need to know their opinions secondhand. I didn't need to hear it through a mutual acquaintance. I had permission to say, *"Please stop relaying messages to me from people who do not love or value me."*

He also reminded me that I had permission not to share. That if I trusted someone with a piece of my heart and they turned it into a conversation with someone else—especially someone who might use it against me—I had every right to draw back. I didn't owe an explanation for distancing myself or holding things closer to the chest. My silence didn't mean guilt—it meant growth. And protecting peace is not the same thing as hiding.

We also talked about expectations. He told me, *"Expectations are just disappointments waiting to happen."* That one line began to change the way I saw my relationships. People were more than willing to remind me of my shortcomings and past failures, or even poke fun at me in front of others to get a laugh or feel relevant, but as my therapist reminded me, no one is perfect. No one can live up to a standard of flawlessness—not me and not them.

When someone continually brings up your past, throws your pain in your face, or embarrasses you to boost their own presence in a room, it's not about you. It reveals something broken in them. According to psychologist Brené Brown, shame thrives in secrecy and silence, and those who shame others are often deflecting their own pain. Public humiliation, she explains, is a tactic people use when they feel powerless or insecure themselves. (Source: Brown, Brené. "*Daring Greatly*," 2012.)

Recognizing that freed me. I didn't have to internalize the things said about me. I also began to realize that many people had expectations of me that they didn't hold for themselves or others. Why? Because it was easier to demand from me than to reflect on their own behavior. As Brené Brown writes, "*We're hard on each other because we're using each other as a launching pad out of our own perceived shaming deficiency.*" (Source: Brown, Brené. "*Daring Greatly*," 2012.)

The truth is, people will often try to keep you where they need you to stay so they don't have to grow. Your growth threatens their comfort. Your boundaries expose their lack of them, and your healing challenges their unwillingness to face their own wounds.

My therapist and I talked a lot about how others' judgments and commentaries—while often framed as helpful—were actually little arrows that pierced deeper wounds. Some people always seemed to have a better way, a corrective word, or a reminder of how I could have done something differently. He reminded me that not every comment deserved a response, and that often, unsolicited advice is just criticism wearing a mask.

One quote my therapist shared became an anchor in my healing—something Brené Brown also references often—words from Theodore Roosevelt:

"It is not the critic who counts; not the man who points out how the strong man stumbles, or where the doer of deeds could have done them better. The credit belongs to the man who is actually in the arena… who errs, who comes up short again and again… but who does actually strive to do the deeds… and who, at the worst, if he fails, at least fails while daring greatly."

I remember sitting at a table with people I once called safe. One moment I was laughing, the next I was the punchline—again. Something I'd once shared privately became the center of a joke, and everyone laughed—including the person I'd trusted with it. I smiled too, but inside I broke a little more. Later, when I brought it up, I was told I was too sensitive, that it was *"just a joke."* My therapist told me that day, *"You don't have to keep handing your heart to people who use it for entertainment."* That was a turning point. I started paying attention to how I felt after interactions. If I left feeling smaller, unheard, or shamed, I started giving myself permission to back away. Quietly, without guilt. I didn't have to carry them anymore. Because God was teaching me to listen for His voice—and His voice doesn't mock or shame. His voice heals.

As I began to heal, not everyone celebrated it. Some criticized the very growth that was saving me. I learned to guard my therapy journey fiercely—not out of secrecy, but out of sacredness. I was changing. God was doing deep work in me, and I knew I needed healing that touched every part of who I was: mind, body, and soul.

That kind of transformation can be uncomfortable for people who aren't ready to face their own brokenness, but I was no longer willing to shrink to keep others comfortable.

I am not my mistakes. I am not my sins. I have made mistakes and I have sinned. But I am no more defined by my past than I am by the salad I ate for lunch. I've heard it said, *"You are what you eat,"* but thank God that's not true—because if it were, I'd be a strong cup of coffee and a handful of dark chocolate! Just like what I eat doesn't determine my identity, neither do the worst things I've done. Grace tells me the truth: I am not what I've done. I am who God says I am.

Let me tell you what also began to shift my perspective during this time: the realization that God has always used broken people. Not perfect people. Not polished people. But people with real, messy pasts. If you've ever read Hebrews 11—sometimes called the *"Hall of Faith"*—you'll see what I mean. It lists people who are considered heroes of faith, those who trusted God and were used mightily by Him, but when you look closer at their stories, you'll notice something extraordinary: they were far from perfect.

Noah got drunk. Abraham lied—more than once. Sarah laughed at God's promise. Jacob was a deceiver. Moses murdered a man. Rahab was a prostitute. David was an adulterer and a murderer. Samson was impulsive and vengeful. Yet here they are—not erased, not dismissed, but honored. Why? Because God's grace has always been greater than human failure.

Hebrews 11:34–35 says, *"Their weakness was turned to strength... Others were tortured, refusing to turn from God in order to be set free. They placed their hope in a better life after the resurrection."*

God didn't use them despite their past—He used them through their past. Their brokenness didn't disqualify them; it became the very backdrop against which His redemption story was written.

If God could still call them worthy of honor, what was I doing disqualifying myself? If He could use someone like David—deeply flawed, yet deeply repentant—then there was still hope for me. There is still hope for you. Because He's still writing redemption stories. And yours isn't finished yet.

📖 Reflection & Renewal: Journal and Action Steps

📜 Scriptures for Meditation:

- **Isaiah 43:18–19** – *"Forget the former things; do not dwell on the past. See, I am doing a new thing!"*

- **Galatians 5:1** – *"It is for freedom that Christ has set us free. Stand firm, then, and do not let yourselves be burdened again by a yoke of slavery."*

- **Psalm 147:3** – *"He heals the brokenhearted and binds up their wounds."*

- **Ephesians 2:10** – *"For we are God's masterpiece. He has created us anew in Christ Jesus, so we can do the good things He planned for us long ago."*

- **Zephaniah 3:17** – *"The Lord your God is with you, the Mighty Warrior who saves. He will take great delight in you... He will rejoice over you with singing."*

✒ Journal Prompts:

1. What lie have I believed about myself because of a past mistake or someone else's words?

2. When in my story, did I start attaching my worth to performance or people-pleasing?

3. What *"roles"* have I played (peacekeeper, overachiever, etc.) that kept me from being my authentic self?

4. What are some phrases or labels others have spoken over me that I need to release?

5. When I replay the *"tape"* of my life, where can I now see God's hand—even in the pain?

6. How can I replace one of the lies I believed with truth from God's Word?

7. Who do I need to set boundaries with, and what does it look like to protect my peace without guilt?

✅ Next Steps to Walk Out Healing

1. Speak one truth aloud from scripture each morning.

2. Set one boundary this week to protect your peace.

3. Replace one condemning thought with God's truth.

4. Celebrate one area where you've seen growth or made a different choice.

You're not just reading a chapter—you're living a breakthrough. Keep going. God's not done with your story. Not even close.

📑 Acknowledgments, Citations & Further Reading:

References for this chapter include excerpts and paraphrased concepts from:

- Brown, Brené. Daring Greatly. 2012.
- Virkler, Mark. *Prayers That Heal the Heart*. Communion With God Ministries, 2001.
- The American Psychological Association – *"Life Review Therapy,"* APA Dictionary of Psychology.
- HelpGuide.org – *"Codependency."*
- The National Domestic Violence Hotline – *"Trauma Bonding."*
- National Child Traumatic Stress Network (NCTSN). *"Sexual Abuse."* www.nctsn.org
- Allender, Dan B. *The Wounded Heart: Hope for Adult Victims of Childhood Sexual Abuse.* NavPress, 2008.
- Brown, Brené. *The Gifts of Imperfection*. Hazelden Publishing, 2010.
- Scripture References: 2 Corinthians 10:5, Psalm 34:18, Romans 8:1, Hebrews 11

For further reading and support:

- *The Body Keeps the Score* by Bessel van der Kolk
- *Try Softer* by Aundi Kolber
- Lerner, Harriet. *The Dance of Connection*. Harper Perennial, 2001.
- Linehan, Marsha M. *"Validation in Psychotherapy and Daily Life."* American Journal of Psychotherapy, 1997
- RAINN (Rape, Abuse & Incest National Network): www.rainn.org | 800.656.HOPE

- Celebrate Recovery: www.celebraterecovery.com
- Christian counselors: www.aacc.net (American Association of Christian Counselors)

You are not your mistakes. You are not what happened to you. You are loved, chosen, redeemed—and healing is possible.

Chapter 4

Overcoming Addiction

Addiction is a word that carries weight, shame, and misunderstanding—and yet, it also carries the potential for redemption. In 2004 and 2005, our home became both a battlefield and a birthplace. A battlefield for the lies, pain, and addiction that threatened to tear our marriage apart… and a birthplace for the restoration that only God could bring.

This is the chapter where things started to break open—where hidden struggles came to light and healing began to take root. It's the story of how God stepped into our chaos with conviction, mercy, and relentless grace. It's the story of the man I love, the battles we faced, and the God who refused to let us go.

I can still remember how the air felt in the summer of 2004. Heavy. Thick. Like something was coming, and I couldn't name it yet. There were whispers in my heart—gut feelings I tried to ignore. I noticed the late nights, the shifting stories, the silence that hung in the spaces between us. At first, I thought maybe there was someone else. Maybe an affair. I prepared myself to discover another woman.

But nothing prepared me for what I actually found.

It wasn't another woman—it was another world. A hidden addiction. Crack cocaine had become the mistress I never saw coming, and with it came a darkness I couldn't have imagined. One that stole not only trust, but identity, security, and sanity. I wasn't just afraid—I was unraveling.

Before I can tell you about the addiction that nearly destroyed us, I have to first tell you how we began. Because our story didn't start with addiction. It started with pain—mine.

I met my husband during one of the most broken seasons of my life. I had just walked away from my first marriage, and not because I didn't believe in commitment. I believed in it so deeply that I stayed longer than I should have. When the relationship crossed a line— when fear became something I could no longer deny—I knew it was time to go. I chose to leave.

I packed up my children and moved into a small townhome, trying to rebuild a life. I was reeling, ashamed, and deeply wounded—not just by the abuse, but by the rejection that followed. The church I had attended, the place where I brought my children to worship and grow, decided that my divorce was a greater sin than the abuse I had endured. They condemned me for leaving. That kind of spiritual betrayal cuts deep.

So, there I was—alone, four kids in tow, carrying a life suitcase stuffed with shame, fear, unworthiness, and a twisted sense of love. I didn't know who I was unless someone else needed me. I measured my value by how useful I could be, how self-sacrificing I could become. Chapter 1 displayed how much I had confused love with performance. Chapter 2 revealed how far removed I was from seeing myself as God did. Chapter 3 demonstrated how desperately

I clung to roles, responsibilities, and relationships that made me feel like I mattered.

When I met him, I wasn't whole. I wasn't healed. I was a woman looking for someone to choose me. To see past my baggage. To make me feel seen.

I just wanted to be loved. Not for what I could do. Not for how I could fix or perform or please. Just... loved.

But here's the truth I couldn't see at the time: when your suitcase is still full of unhealed wounds, even the sincerest love can get tangled in the contents. And sometimes, you don't realize what's packed in there until it spills all over the floor.

He was charming. Funny. The life of the party. The kind of man who made everyone laugh—especially when the drinks were flowing. He had a presence about him, like he was trying to fill every room he walked into. I saw the brokenness, though I didn't know how deep it went. He drank heavily, but it was always in the name of fun. Social. Harmless, I told myself. After all, who was I to judge anyone for not having it all together?

He had two small daughters and said he wanted family—something real, something rooted. That word—family—hooked my heart. He saw my children and didn't run. Instead, he leaned in. He made me feel chosen. Safe. Wanted.

But what I didn't realize at the time was that both of us were showing up with full suitcases. He had his, and I had mine. The baggage we hadn't named. Hurts that hadn't healed. The lies we believed about ourselves.

At that time, I couldn't see how wounded he was. That the drinking wasn't just partying—it was numbing. That the need to be the life of the party was masking a lifetime of pain. That under all that laughter and bravado was a man who, like me, was searching for identity, worth, and safety.

We came together not as two whole people, but as two survivors trying to build something steady on top of shattered places. And in those early days, it felt like maybe love could fix what was broken.

But love alone doesn't heal what hasn't been faced.

And unhealed people don't stay stagnant—they either break down or break open.

I had no idea what I was stepping into—and to be fair, neither did he. We both came with pasts, but we also had very real, very messy presents. Little lives were counting on us to figure it out. To hold it together. To make something work from the wreckage.

I saw areas that I could help. Places I could fix, patch, or mend. I stepped in with the full force of my heart—ready to mom, support, and, let's be honest… rescue. Because that's what I did. If I could hold up all the broken pieces, maybe—just maybe—we could build something solid.

What we hadn't counted on was just how loud the chaos around us would become. It felt like we were juggling flaming swords while smiling for the neighborhood cookout.

And every day, I slipped further into survival mode.

But underneath the chaos, under the court dates, the screaming matches, the substance abuse, and the silence… was a deep ache in both of us. We weren't just fighting our circumstances, we were fighting our unhealed wounds, our old identities, our need to be needed, and the lies we believed about love, worth, and God.

We were building a life on broken ground, and eventually, the cracks began to show.

Before the cracks appeared, there were already two separate wars quietly waging—one rooted in absence, and one rooted in broken trust.

On one side, I carried the deep ache of unfulfilled promises—the weight of what was missing, the questions left unanswered, the gaps no human effort could ever fully bridge. I tried to shield my children from the wounds that weren't mine to heal, often feeling like I was fighting a battle no one could see.

On the other side, there was a history heavy with hurt and misunderstanding. Attempts to build a stable, safe home were constantly challenged by old wounds that refused to stay buried. Court battles, misunderstandings, and the echoes of past pain spilled over into the present, making even simple days feel like uphill climbs.

There was no handbook for this kind of healing.
No step-by-step plan for how to build peace out of broken pieces.

But here is what I know now: Even in the wreckage, God was working.
Even in the silence, He was speaking.
Even when it felt like all I could see was the debris of what should have been, He was already weaving together a future full of hope.

We were surviving—but He was preparing us to thrive.
And while the battles were real, His grace was greater.
Every tear shed, every prayer whispered, every quiet step forward was seen, and gathered up into His plan to redeem, restore, and rebuild.

According to the National Association for Children of Alcoholics, more than 26.8 million children in the United States are exposed to alcoholism or substance abuse in their families. Children in these households are significantly more likely to experience mental health challenges, academic struggles, and long-term relational dysfunction.

Celebrate Recovery, a Christ-centered recovery program, reports that two-thirds of its participants are not dealing with drugs or alcohol at all. They're showing up for codependency, abuse, depression, eating disorders, trauma, and grief. The root issues go deeper than substance; they are spiritual, emotional, and relational.

Addiction doesn't just knock on one door. It walks through the whole house. It seeps into the foundation, and unless it's addressed with truth, grace, and help, it will rot everything in its path.

Our house—our hearts—were no exception.

The cracks weren't just forming—they were splitting everything wide open, and it wouldn't be long before everything came to a head.

I could write ten books on the toll addiction takes—not just on the addict, but on everyone who loves them. I could tell you stories that would make you cry. I could paint pictures of the truly devastating and heartbreaking face of addiction. Just know that if you can imagine it—we've probably seen it. But that isn't what this chapter is about. Yes, I want to help you understand where we were. Yes, it took a toll on our family, and in some ways—many ways—the repercussions are still felt in some of our lives more than others. The key here is that we had a *BUT GOD* experience.

A *BUT GOD* experience is what happens when everything should have fallen apart—when the world says it's over, when the odds are stacked against you, when there's no logical reason for restoration or hope... and then God steps in. It's the moment when heaven interrupts the downward spiral with His mercy, His power, and His purpose. It's when bondage meets breakthrough. It's when the past doesn't get the final word because His grace rewrites the ending.

Addiction wears many faces. While society often focuses on substances like alcohol and drugs, it's crucial to recognize that addiction can manifest in behaviors that seem harmless—or even praised—on the surface. These behavioral addictions can be just as consuming and destructive.

Common behavioral addictions include:

- **Gambling:** An uncontrollable urge to gamble despite harmful consequences.
- **Food:** Binge eating or using food to cope emotionally.
- **Shopping:** Compulsive buying to ease emotional distress.
- **Work:** Workaholism that strains relationships and self-worth.
- **Exercise:** Obsessive exercising leading to physical and emotional strain.
- **Social media & the Internet:** Excessive use that disrupts healthy routines.
- **Sex & Pornography:** Compulsive behaviors that impair intimacy and stability.

According to American Addiction Centers and Valley Spring Recovery, these addictions stimulate the brain's reward system in much the same way as drugs and alcohol, creating a cycle of compulsion and distress. Celebrate Recovery teaches that recovery isn't just about substance—it's about uncovering the root, healing the wound, and walking forward in freedom.

In our journey, we had to look beyond just the visible addiction. We had to open our eyes to all the ways pain was playing out—and surrender every single one to the One who heals.

Surrender came in May of 2005. I collapsed in tears at 1 AM in the middle of my front yard. It was so muggy—the air was thick, and I could feel it weighing me down as I sank to the ground. The dew had already started to form, and between the heaviness of the air, the steady stream of tears, and the wet grass beneath me, I was drenched. I was suffocating in the thickness of everything around me and everything happening in me. My husband was on a binge, and I just couldn't take it anymore. I was at the very end of my rope—physically, emotionally, and spiritually depleted. I wrongly believed that if I just said the right thing, did the right thing, or pleaded hard enough, he would change.

That's the trap of codependency, especially within the heart of addiction. It's a twisted dance of trying to save someone who doesn't want to be saved. You start thinking their healing is your responsibility. Their choices are somehow your fault. You absorb their pain and let it shape your identity.

Codependency in addiction can look like enabling, people-pleasing, self-neglect, and obsessively focusing on the addict's needs while ignoring your own. You lose your sense of self while trying to hold someone else together. It is love distorted by fear. It's a survival mechanism wrapped in false hope.

I didn't know it then, but I had become addicted to his recovery. To his potential. To the hope that one day he would wake up and see the light, and all this heartache would be worth it. But that night in the yard was the beginning of my surrender. A holy breaking point.

What I haven't yet shared is what happened just before I collapsed in the yard that night. I had just returned from a bar—one of the rougher ones in town—where a friend had driven me to find my husband. He had taken our truck after I told him, plainly and firmly, that if he did, I was done. That I would come for it. For him. For us. And when the call came that he was drinking and using again—that they had taken the truck and gone—I knew he had called my bluff.

I walked into that bar to get the keys and ask him to come home. He laughed in my face. They all did. Even the friend who drove me there sat down and ordered a drink. In that moment, something broke inside of me. I walked outside and called the police, begging them to help me. When they walked in and returned with the keys, they offered no other meaningful assistance. The truck was many blocks away. One officer looked at me—hysterical, scared, completely unraveled—and, finally, relented and gave me a ride. I drove that truck home—numb, exhausted, and shattered. That's when I fell into the yard.

Grass clung to my face. My clothes were soaked with dew and tears. I had nothing left to give. He came home a few hours later, very high, very drunk, and very mad. I woke the kids and walked to a neighbor's house. When the sun rose, and while the kids slept safely inside her home, I called my parents and asked them to come. In the driveway of my friend's home, I poured out the story of what had been hiding behind closed doors. I was broken, sobbing, and needing a miracle.

My parents and I walked back down to our house, and for the next ten hours, we had an intervention. It began with a storm of angry emotions and harsh *"get out"* declarations, but ended with my father leading my husband in the sinner's prayer—inviting him to surrender the demons destroying him to the only One who could truly set him free.

We began attending daily recovery meetings. We read the Bible together. We prayed together. We sat in circles of strangers who understood the madness. It wasn't pretty at first. We were in and out of Narcotics Anonymous and Alcoholics Anonymous meetings. We found a faith-based 12-step program. That's where things truly began to shift.

There, in the presence of God's grace, we laid our hang-ups, habits, addictions, and heartache at the foot of the cross. God placed some incredible people in our lives that night—people who would become trusted friends, turned family. True *"ride or die"* at all the levels that matter. My surrender may have started that night in the middle of my front yard—but my recovery began right alongside his, at the foot of the cross. That week, I attended my first recovery meeting. I wrote down every dark secret, every fear, every thread of shame and guilt on slips of paper—and I nailed them to the cross. I picked up my first white chip, surrendering to recovery from codependency.

Recovery from codependency is not about fixing the addict. It's about healing yourself. According to Christian counselors and authors like Melody Beattie and biblical scholars like Henry Cloud, it means learning to set boundaries, recognizing enabling behaviors, and finding your identity in Christ—not in someone else's choices. As Brené Brown says, *"When we deny our stories, they define us. When we own our stories, we get to write the ending."*

I was learning, one small act at a time, that I didn't have to carry the weight of someone else's healing. I could surrender my part, trust God with theirs, and start walking toward wholeness.

On July 4th of 2005, my husband picked up his surrender chip. As of the writing of this book, we are looking forward to celebrating 20 years of him being clean and set free—July 4th, 2025! It marks his dependence on God for true freedom. The day he was set free and given a new life wasn't just a turning point—it was a spiritual resurrection—a declaration of God's power to redeem what was once completely lost. It marked the breaking of chains. When he accepted God's free gift of salvation, every generational curse was broken. The blood of the Lamb will do that.

The journey since 2005 has not been easy. The enemy of our souls and homes has shot many a fiery arrow our way. It has been filled with setbacks and setups, but despite all of those, it has also been filled with progress, redemption, recovery, and reconciliation. Healing isn't a one-and-done process. Healing is a daily choice—cemented with daily habits, daily decisions, taking every thought captive, and deciding to do the next right thing. It has meant dying to self while putting God and each other first. Healing will be a daily action step until we meet our Savior face to face. What we hold tight to is our need for a Savior, and that God must become first in our lives. We must recognize that when He does life with us, it's a life worth living.

We have been granted opportunities to share our testimony over these past years—how God took our mess and turned it into a message of His goodness. You *CAN* and *WILL* recover. You are *NOT* your mistakes. You are *NOT* your past. You are *NOT* an addict. You are a daughter and a son of God, the Most High. You are royalty. You are called and set apart. The enemy knows it, or he wouldn't be working overtime to take you *OUT* along with those who love you. He knows your legacy is powerful, and he wants to stop you in your tracks.

This is where we cry out and surrender. This is where we let go of trying it our way. This is where we recognize the insanity of doing the same thing day in and day out, expecting a new result. In our strength, we cannot do it. Sure, maybe for a while. After all, we probably all know a *"dry drunk"*, but in Christ, recovery is different. It won't be easy, but it will be freeing—and He will redeem the years the locusts ate away.

Again, make no mistake—recovery isn't a one-time event. It's a day-by-day, moment-by-moment way of life. You can only break free from the chains that bind you by making lasting changes in your mind, your emotions, and your soul. You need to change your thinking—thought by thought, second by second. You begin to create space—just ten seconds, sometimes—to breathe, to process, and to choose the next right thing.

Recovery demands change. You change your people, your places, and your things. You surround yourself with people who have walked the walk and have real clean time under their belt—people who will pour truth and encouragement into you. You show up, even when you don't feel like it. And, prayerfully, your entire family needs to take this journey with you.

Because addiction is not just the addict's issue—it is a family disease. It touches everyone. True healing only happens when the whole house begins to recover. Recovery for the family is just as important as it is for the one using. Without it, old patterns creep back in. Enabling returns. Trust erodes. But, with it—intentional healing for the spouse, the kids, the home—God brings full restoration. Not perfection. But peace. Not forgetting, but freedom. It starts with surrender... every single day.

There is also hope for children growing up in addicted households— real, documented, transformational hope. When families begin the work of recovery together—engaging in counseling, faith-based support, and open communication—children can and do heal.

According to research published in the *Journal of Substance Abuse Treatment*, children who participate in structured family recovery programs show significant improvement in emotional resilience, academic success, and long-term relational stability.

Christian-based programs such as Celebrate Recovery's *"Celebration Place"* and *"The Landing"* are designed specifically to support children and teens affected by addiction in the home. These programs equip young people with faith, tools, and language to process their emotions, develop healthy coping strategies, and build trust with safe adults.

The healing of the family starts with honesty, with surrender, and with the unwavering belief that God can redeem every broken part.

Momma or Daddy, reading this right now—this is for you. If your child has been exposed to addiction, know this: there is hope. You are not powerless to change the narrative. Children in addicted homes don't have to be defined by the trauma. With truth, safety, and love, healing happens.

Studies show that protective factors—supportive adults, faith-based community, counseling, and routine—can help children build resilience even in the face of adversity. According to the Harvard Center on the Developing Child, the presence of a stable, caring adult is the single most powerful buffer against lifelong damage from toxic stress.

You may feel like you've already messed everything up, but listen: repair is always possible. The very act of acknowledging what your child has lived through is the beginning of that repair. Recovery for your family includes their voice, their emotions, and their need for safety. And when that space is created? Healing takes root.

Don't just survive this. Recover together. Invite your children into the healing. Give them language. Give them permission to grieve and grow. Let them see you get help, and remind them that broken doesn't mean beyond repair. God is the healer of generations—and it starts with one decision to say, "*It ends with me.*"

The importance of family healing in addiction recovery is more than a hopeful sentiment—it's backed by research and widely recognized by treatment professionals. According to the Substance Abuse and Mental Health Services Administration (SAMHSA), involving family in recovery increases treatment retention and outcomes. In fact, family therapy is considered a critical part of recovery because addiction disrupts the emotional, relational, and spiritual health of the entire family system.

Dr. Claudia Black, a pioneer in family addiction therapy, has long emphasized that "*addiction is a family disease and recovery is a family process.*" Left unaddressed, the wounds of addiction become generational, but when the whole family engages in healing— through support groups, counseling, and faith-based recovery programs—restoration becomes a reality.

A 2018 study published in the Journal of Groups in Addiction & Recovery states that recovery efforts are more sustainable when the family is involved because they help rebuild communication, restore trust, and support accountability.

Faith-based programs like Celebrate Recovery and Hope Christian Ministries recognize this deeply. They encourage family members to attend groups for codependency, anger, and trauma—not just substance use. Healing multiplies when everyone is doing the work.

Addiction thrives in isolation, but healing happens in connection. For our family, it started when we all said yes to the process. Together.

Forgiveness and grace became the foundation on which our healing could be built. When my husband called me the day after the intervention—broken and pleading for forgiveness—I had a decision to make. Voice trembling, he said he needed me. Our kids needed us. He couldn't fight this battle alone. He begged me to let him come home and walk through recovery with him. This was another suitcase moment. I had to decide what I was still willing to carry—and what I was ready to lay down. This was when I realized healing wouldn't come through pretending everything was fine, but by choosing grace and truth, even when it hurt.

And I chose to forgive him. Not halfway. Not conditionally. Not until the next fight or the next trigger or the next slip-up. I chose forgiveness. Full stop. Because if I was going to live what I claimed to believe—about grace, redemption, and second chances—I had to forgive myself, and my husband as well.

That didn't mean there weren't boundaries. It didn't mean trust wasn't something we had to rebuild from the ground up. It absolutely was. Forgiveness is not the same as trust. Forgiveness is a gift; trust is earned. Part of our healing meant putting an action plan on paper—what daily life would look like, what accountability would be in place, and how we would support each other while holding space for hard conversations.

One thing I knew for certain: I would not spend the rest of our marriage weaponizing his past. I would not hold an anvil over his head, reminding him of every wrong. That wasn't grace. That wasn't healing. That would've made me the jailer of a man already walking free.

Forgiveness, according to theologian Lewis Smedes, *"is to set a prisoner free and discover the prisoner was you."* I didn't want to carry the bitterness. I wanted freedom for both of us.

Research backs this up. According to a study published in the *Journal of Family Psychology* (Fincham, Hall, & Beach, 2006), couples who practice true forgiveness experience greater emotional healing and marital satisfaction. Not because they forget, but because they choose not to keep score.

Scripture reminds us, *"Be kind and compassionate to one another, forgiving each other, just as in Christ God forgave you."* – Ephesians 4:32.

God had forgiven me. Countless times. If I wanted healing to flow in our home, I had to extend that same grace. It was a blind step of faith, but it was the very thing that changed everything. Forgiveness didn't mean I condoned what happened—it meant I was choosing to release it, and not let it become the soundtrack of our future. I wanted freedom for my husband, but I needed it for myself, too.

And it began the day I said: *"Yes. Come home. We will figure this out together."*

Biblical Recovery Principles from Celebrate Recovery

Celebrate Recovery is a Christ-centered 12-step program that aligns each traditional recovery step with a biblical principle and scripture. Here are the 8 Recovery Principles based on the Beatitudes:

1. **Realize I'm not God.** I admit that I am powerless to control my tendency to do the wrong thing and that my life is unmanageable.

"Blessed are the poor in spirit, for theirs is the kingdom of heaven." – Matthew 5:3

2. **Earnestly believe that God exists,** that I matter to Him, and that He has the power to help me recover.

   "Blessed are those who mourn, for they shall be comforted." – Matthew 5:4

3. **Consciously choose to commit all my life and will to Christ's care and control.**

   "Blessed are the meek, for they shall inherit the earth." – Matthew 5:5

4. **Openly examine and confess my faults** to myself, to God, and to someone I trust.

   "Blessed are the pure in heart, for they shall see God." – Matthew 5:8

5. **Voluntarily submit to every change** God wants to make in my life and humbly ask Him to remove my character defects.

   "Blessed are those who hunger and thirst for righteousness, for they shall be filled." – Matthew 5:6

6. **Evaluate all my relationships.** Offer forgiveness to those who have hurt me and make amends for harm I've done to others.

   "Blessed are the merciful, for they shall obtain mercy."

– Matthew 5:7

7. **Reserve a daily time with God** for self-examination, Bible reading, and prayer in order to know God and His will for my life.

   "Blessed are the peacemakers, for they shall be called children of God." – Matthew 5:9

8. **Yield myself to God** to be used to bring this Good News to others, both by my example and by my words.

   "Blessed are those who are persecuted because of righteousness, for theirs is the kingdom of heaven." – Matthew 5:10

Biblical 12 Steps

1) We admitted we were powerless over our addictions and compulsive behaviors, that our lives had become unmanageable.

   I know that nothing good lives in me, that is, in my sinful nature. For I have the desire to do what is good, but I cannot carry it out. - Romans 7:18

2) *We came to believe that a power greater than ourselves could*

   For it is God who works in you to will and to act according to his good purpose. - Philippians 2:13

3) We made a decision to turn our lives and our wills over to the care of God.

> *Therefore, I urge you, brothers, in view of God's mercy, to offer your bodies as living sacrifices, holy and pleasing to God – this is your spiritual act of worship. - Romans 12:1*

4) We made a searching and fearless moral inventory of ourselves.

> *Let us examine our ways and test them, and let us return to the Lord. - Lamentations 3:40*

5) We admitted to God, to ourselves, and to another human being the exact nature of our wrongs.

> *Therefore, confess your sins to each other and pray for each other so that you may be healed. - James 5:16*

6) We were entirely ready to have God remove all these defects of character.

> *Humble yourselves before the Lord, and he will lift you up.*
> *- James 4:10*

7) We humbly asked Him to remove all our shortcomings.

> *If we confess our sins, he is faithful and will forgive us our sins and purify us from all unrighteousness. - 1 John 1:9*

8) We made a list of all persons we had harmed and became willing to make amends to them all.

Do to others as you would have them do to you. - Luke 6:31

9) We made direct amends to such people whenever possible, except when to do so would injure them or others.

Therefore, if you are offering your gift at the altar and there remember that your brother has something against you, leave your gift there in front of the altar. First go and be reconciled to your brother; then come and offer your gift. - Matthew 5:23-24

10) We continue to take personal inventory and when we were wrong, promptly admitted it.

So, if you think you are standing firm, be careful that you don't fall! - 1 Corinthians 10:12

11) We sought through prayer and meditation to improve our conscious contact with God, praying only for knowledge of His will for us, and power to carry that out.

Let the word of Christ dwell in you richly. - Colossians 3:16

12) Having had a spiritual experience as the result of these steps, we try to carry this message to others and practice these principles in all our affairs.

Brothers, if someone is caught in a sin, you who are spiritual should restore them gently. But watch yourself, or you also may be tempted. - Galatians 6:1

📖 Reflection & Renewal: Journal and Action Steps

📃 Scripture for Meditation:

- *"Come to me, all you who are weary and burdened, and I will give you rest."* – Matthew 11:28

- *"So, if the Son sets you free, you will be free indeed."* – John 8:36

- *"He heals the brokenhearted and binds up their wounds."* – Psalm 147:3

- *"You intended to harm me, but God intended it for good…"* – Genesis 50:20

- *"I will repay you for the years the locusts have eaten…"* – Joel 2:25

✎ Journal Prompts:

Use the space below to begin processing your story, identifying areas where surrender is needed, and calling out the next step God is asking you to take.

1. What areas of your life have you tried to control, fix, or carry on your own strength?

2. How has addiction—your own or someone else's— 'impacted your emotional, mental, or spiritual health?

3. In what ways have you enabled or been enabled? What patterns do you see?

4. What would it look like to truly surrender? Who do you need to invite into your healing journey?

5. Are there boundaries you need to set—or voices you need to quiet—to walk in recovery?

6. What does freedom look like to you? What is one small next step toward that freedom?

Write honestly. Pray boldly. Cry out if you need to. God meets us in the middle of the mess—and leads us toward restoration.

✅ Next Steps to Walk Out Healing

- **Pick Up Your White Chip (Spiritually):**
  You don't have to wait for a meeting to surrender. Take a symbolic action today: write down your addiction, hurt, habit, or hang-up and lay it before God in prayer. Place it at the cross—literally or symbolically—and declare, "*I am not this struggle. I am a child of God.*"

- **Create a Recovery Circle:**
  Identify 3–5 people who can be part of your safe space—mentors, prayer partners, friends in faith, or recovery. These are the people you can text, call, cry with, or celebrate clean days with. Recovery happens in the community.

- **Make a Family Healing Plan:**
  Whether your whole household is in recovery or not, map out how healing can start where you are. Who needs counseling? Where can safety be reinforced? What rhythms (prayer, dinner, journaling) need to be prioritized?

- **Set a "*Just for Today*" Intention:**
  Just for today—choose truth. Choose one new behavior, one new prayer, and one safe boundary. Don't worry about tomorrow yet. Just for today, walk in freedom.

- **Name Your Triggers. Build Your Tools:**
  List your top emotional or environmental triggers. Write down a grace-based response or escape route for each. Use Scripture, affirmations, or trusted contacts to redirect in real time when temptation hits.

- **Celebrate Clean Moments, Not Just Clean Time:**
  Whether it's one day, one week, or one hard conversation handled in love—mark it. Journal it. Praise God for it. Don't wait for perfection to celebrate progress.

🖹 Acknowledgments, Citations & Further Reading:

Finding Help and Hope in Recovery:

- If you or someone you love is battling addiction—substance or behavioral—know that you are not alone. Healing is possible.
- Consider reaching out to your local church or faith-based support networks.
- **Celebrate Recovery** is a nationwide Christ-centered recovery program offering support for a wide range of hurts, habits, and hang-ups. Learn more and find a group near you at www.celebraterecovery.com.
- **Hope Christian Ministries (HOPE CM)** offers biblically grounded resources and recovery tools for individuals and families seeking healing through Jesus Christ. Learn more at www.hopecm.com.
- **SAMHSA's National Helpline** (1-800-662-HELP) provides free, confidential, 24/7 treatment referral and information for individuals and families facing mental and/or substance use disorders.
- Smedes, Lewis B. *Forgive and Forget: Healing the Hurts We Don't Deserve.* HarperOne, 2007. (Referenced for the quote: *"To forgive is to set a prisoner free and discover the prisoner was you."*)
- Fincham, F. D., Hall, J. H., & Beach, S. R. H. (2006). *"Forgiveness in Marriage: Current Status and Future Directions." Journal of Family Psychology,* 20(2), 143–153. https://doi.org/10.1037/0893-3200.20.2.143

Portions of this chapter were informed by research and publicly available content from:

- National Association for Children of Alcoholics –
  www.nacoa.org
- Celebrate Recovery – www.celebraterecovery.com
- American Addiction Centers –
  www.americanaddictioncenters.org
- Valley Spring Recovery Center –
  www.valleyspringrecovery.com

These resources provide additional insight into the family impact of addiction, behavioral addictions, and recovery through faith and support. For a complete list of sources referenced in this book, please see the Acknowledgments & Citations section at the back.

Chapter 5
Don't Let My Hand Go

Healing isn't linear. It's not a neat checklist. It's not a perfect arc. Healing is a journey that winds through surrender and suffering, joy and heartbreak, and when you think you've unpacked all the pain, a new chapter shows up that will force you to go even deeper.

By the time summer of 2020 arrived, I had faced addiction, codependency, identity, and loss. I had begun laying my suitcase open before God—to let Him repack it with truth, grace, and love. But nothing could have prepared me for what was coming next.

This is the chapter where my faith had to rise—not as a sentiment, but as a survival tool.

This is the chapter where God didn't just show up in my healing, He showed up in my crisis.

June 23, 2020, it was 12:15. I had spent the morning in Suffolk, VA, showing homes to two new clients, conducting a walk-through for a closing with another client, and a home inspection for yet another. It was a busy day, in a busy week, with nine clients in various stages of the home buying process. My husband and I had been remodeling our house. Truthfully, he did the work, while I did the planning, selections, and spending—Amazon's big blue swoosh was the logo, and Wayfair's *"got just what I need"* was the soundtrack. Erick was off to find a plumbing part and had stopped at the Ocean Front to call me back before heading home. We planned to meet back at home and have lunch before heading to the flooring company to pick out transition strips. We had a plan! I would drive from Suffolk, and he would head home from Virginia Beach, and we should meet in about 30–40 minutes.

In my mind, I was looking forward to one of those sweet, simple afternoons we had grown to cherish. The kind that slips by almost unnoticed if you're not careful, but later becomes the moment you wish you could relive over and over. We had plans—not grand ones—just the kind that make a house feel like a home and a life that feels grounded. Lunch together, something light—maybe a sandwich and chips on the porch. We'd pick out those transition strips for the flooring project we had been slowly tackling between work and life. The new floors were finally coming together—one box of planks and one YouTube tutorial at a time. Afterward, we'd sit on the front swing with iced coffees in hand—mine with almond milk and his with cream. We'd listen to the birds, maybe talk about what was left on the remodel list, or more honestly, what else was on my honey-do list. It was a normal day—mundane in the best kind of way. That's the thing about trauma... it always shows up uninvited, right in the middle of the ordinary.

I got home and started writing an offer. Time passed, and then he called. I said, *"You're late."* He said nothing. I spoke his name, figuring he had pocket dialed me as he was on his motorcycle. After saying his name a few times, a woman said, *"Ma'am?"* *"Ummm, yes?"* I replied. I don't recall her name, just that she calmly said my husband had been in a motorcycle accident and they were checking him out, and if I could make my way to the hospital at my earliest convenience. *"Yes, of course, I am on my way."* I hung up, grabbed my purse, and jumped in my Jeep. Strangely calm yet breaking all kinds of laws, I made my way to the hospital. I had prayed the whole ride, and pulling in the parking spot realized I better call someone to let them know where I was and why. Not knowing what I was going to find when I walked in, I just needed someone to know. I called my mom as I stepped out of the jeep. I don't recall her words. I walked into the lobby of the ER, and a woman greeted me and asked how she could help me. I said I had received a call, and before I could finish my sentence, two others said, *"Yes, ma'am, we will take you back."*

As they led me down the hall, I remember hearing many people talking. I remember thinking, *"Dear God, please let that not be my husband they are talking about."* A nurse placed her hand gently on my back and said, *"Right this way,"* as the dozen people standing outside a room moved. It was his room.

I can still see it in my head—four surgeons at the foot and to the left side of my husband' bed. He was mostly covered in a sheet, but there was blood. His leg was wrapped, his clothes had been cut off, and he wasn't moving. His eyes were closed. Even as I write this, I can smell the sterile, metallic scent of the room and blood. The horrible smell of blood. If you know, I am very sorry that you know. I can feel how the air left my lungs and the oxygen disappeared from that space. I can feel how hot it was—thick and suffocating. Orders flew from every direction. The sound was deafening, yet it was as if I was watching it in slow motion from far away.

Someone placed his belongings in my hand and said gently, *"Ma'am, please take his ring and his things. You can talk to him quickly. He has to go to surgery."*

I thought I was going to vomit. Or pass out. Or both. Inside, I was screaming. Outside, I began to sob. The surgeon explained what was about to happen. Then he quickly asked someone to escort me to the waiting room. I have no recollection of how I got there. I don't remember who arrived first. I only remember opening my eyes and seeing my family—my mom, my dad, my oldest son. And then a sea of people. At least 20, maybe more—our children, friends, family.

Hours passed like a blur. I can hardly remember conversations. I vaguely remember praying—whispers, pieces of thoughts, a desperate cry for God to do something. It was as if time had frozen and sped up all at once. I was somewhere between numb and nauseous.

When the surgeon came out, his words were clear. *"We're not sure we can save his leg."*

And just like that, everything around me faded. Words exploded like bombs in my mind. My chest tightened. I couldn't breathe. The air left the room. Again.

Remember—this was 2020. COVID restrictions were in place. I don't know how they even let all of these people into the waiting room. Well, that's not entirely true. I do know. God did it. As the security officer began to disperse my loved ones, I was left alone, waiting for them to escort me to the ICU. I had no concept of how long I waited. Time didn't tick—it just suspended itself.

When they finally let me see him, I was escorted into a room full of tubes and wires. Machines were beeping. Lights were blinking. Monitors were glowing softly. And there he was—sedated, still, quiet.

Here's something I've learned: the body will protect us in moments of trauma. A biological grace kicks in when our hearts can't comprehend what's happening. Our nervous system goes into overdrive, buffering shock with numbness. It's God's mercy, I believe. A holy anesthesia that keeps us from breaking wide open too soon.

As I stood beside my husband in that moment—tubes in his arms, machines breathing for him—I was reminded again that healing doesn't begin when the wounds close—but only when the body and soul begin to feel safe enough to process. and for us, that meant facing another battle beneath the surface.

As you know, my husband is a recovered addict. He's walked the long road of sobriety for many years. Over time, whenever pain medication was necessary, we always worked together to create a pain management plan—one grounded in trust, open communication, and accountability. But hospitals don't always understand that. Once you share a history of addiction, providers often get nervous. Some assume absolutely no meds; others overcompensate or don't take it seriously enough.

But here's the truth: sobriety doesn't mean he doesn't feel pain. It doesn't mean he doesn't need medication—it means we use wisdom. Checks. Balances. And compassion. We had to advocate for him more than once during this stay.

My husband hates hospitals. Always has. So, when he began to wake up, still in a fog, disoriented and confused, he didn't know where he was. He didn't understand why he was there. And he didn't know what had happened to his body. That moment of panic, that thrashing confusion, was like watching a trauma unfold inside another trauma. It was terrifying, but it was also human. It reminded me how far we'd come—and how far we still had to walk together.

They insisted I could not stay. He insisted he would not stay without me. At this point, he had no idea what had happened to him, or that we would have just days to make one of the hardest decisions of his life. I tried to explain to the nurse that leaving wasn't what was best for my husband—not for his mental health or his physical recovery. We went around and around, asking to speak to someone higher up, someone who might understand. It went on for hours. I kept pleading. He kept gripping my hand.

It was nearly midnight when the nurse returned and said, "*For right now, I need you to go. But you can come back in three hours. And when you return, you'll be given a badge. From that point forward, you can stay. For as long as he's here, you can stay.*"

We cried. He held my hand so tightly, and we cried. I left around 1:00 a.m., barely remembering the drive home. I showered, changed into fresh clothes, packed a small bag, and set my alarm for 3:00. By 4:00 a.m., I was back in the ICU beside my husband, where I was meant to be.

Every 24 hours for the next three days, he had to undergo another surgery. The surgeons were trying everything—delicately, urgently—hoping to stabilize the damage before we had to face the ultimate question: Did he want to pursue the attempt to save his leg? His leg. To save it would include cadaver bone and cadaver skin to replace what the road had taken.

I won't share the graphic details—only this: We were told to prepare for a transfer to Norfolk General and to anticipate up to 25–30 surgeries over the next year if they were to try to save his leg with a zero guarantee that any of it would actually work and with certainty he would live with pain. We looked at each other and cried. He turned to me, pale and fragile, and said, "*Leslie, there is no way. I can't.*" And all I could whisper back was, "*I know.*"

The surgeons rotated in and out constantly. A vascular specialist assessed whether blood flow could even be maintained. A trauma surgeon managed the ongoing wound care. Infectious disease doctors monitored the threat of severe blood and bone infections. A neurosurgeon evaluated the fractures across his skull and eye socket. Each team brought updates, terms, scans, and scenarios that completely overwhelmed us.

It was too much—too much for anyone to bear, and yet, by the grace of God, we kept breathing.

On Day 4, the surgeon who had worked on his leg came in and offered us some perspective. He wanted us to meet a few men who had faced this decision themselves. During the day, they visited our room: two had lost a leg, one had tried to save it. Each of them came with stories. With scars. With hard-earned wisdom. It's hard to explain what those conversations felt like—sacred, sobering, surreal. For me, I felt helpless. I had spent my whole life trying to fix everything for everyone. But here? I couldn't fix this. I couldn't take the pain away. I couldn't undo what had been done. All I could do was sit beside him, hold his hand, and cry. I could say the name of Jesus—and that was about all I could say before the tears choked out the rest.

Then came Day 5. The talk we knew, and dreaded, was coming. The surgeon had asked me twice if I wanted to be the one to make the call, because we weren't sure how much my husband was comprehending at that point. But I couldn't. I couldn't be the one. It had to be his decision.

So, we started the day with prayer. Together, we made the decision—he made the decision—to let go of his leg and learn to walk again with a prosthetic. Before dinner that day, a wonderful team from REACH Orthotics came in. Matt walked in, not just with a bag, but with hope.

And I want to pause here. Because writing about someone you love losing a limb feels impossible to do without sounding like it's somehow harder on you than on them. It's not. I will never pretend to understand the pain and loss my husband felt in that moment, but I can tell you this: I saw the cost. I saw the courage and hope step through that hospital door wearing scrubs, ready to walk beside him into a brand-new chapter.

I should share that we had no health insurance. Both of us had been healthy, and we decided to pay as we went. Who knew that one elderly woman running a stop sign would change our lives forever? The night of the accident, I didn't know what to do. I called our attorney and dear friend, Hunter. I cried. I don't remember saying anything other than, *"Help me."* He called and said I would meet his friend during my husband's next surgery.

I won't go into specifics about our case, only this: part of our care team became a group of compassionate attorneys that God knew I would need—people who stepped into the chaos and helped handle things far beyond my wheelhouse. They brought calm where there was confusion, clarity where there was fear, and support when I had no idea what to do next.

So, when Matt walked through the door talking like he had a plan, I had to trust that maybe—just maybe—that that plan included a miracle. Matt talked us through the process from the time they took my husband's leg. Then he pulled from his bag a $30,000 foot. Yup. You read that right. I just sank back and started to cry. God, there is no way we can afford for Erick to walk. We don't have that kind of money for extensive prosthetic care. Matt sensed my fear and gently explained that donors would cover this initial cost. All that was required was to get health insurance right away so future needs would be covered. You guessed it—we cried.

The next morning, my husband went in for the removal of what remained of his foot and leg. How do I even begin to explain the emotion here? It's the kind of moment that language fails to hold. I felt a stillness in my chest that wasn't peace—it was the breathlessness of watching someone you love walk toward an irreversible loss. It was grief wrapped in sterile sheets and fluorescent light. I had to be strong, but I was shattered. I had to be present. I wanted to run, yet I stayed. We prayed. We trusted each other. We had no choice but to let go of what we could not change.

Within just a few days, things went from bad to worse. Who knew the roads of Virginia Beach weren't clean? Every type of bone and blood infection one could imagine was now coursing through his body. The medical team went back in three more times, removing more and more bone from his leg in hopes of reaching the infection's edge and saving his life. He was so very sick. Weak. Fragile. I could see the toll it was taking on him. It was terrifying.

Each day, a loved one would drop off food for me, clean clothes, handwritten letters, cards, and little gifts. These small offerings became holy reminders—we were not alone. Each evening, as Erick rested, I would pore through the cards and notes, read the Word aloud, and play praise music softly in our room. We created an atmosphere where the Prince of Peace reigned. Not because we weren't terrified—we were—but because we had no rope to hold on to. We learned many years ago that it is only in Him we live and move, and have our being (Acts 17:28). Worship wasn't a warm fuzzy—it was warfare. It was total surrender. It was our oxygen.

On this particular night, he was so frail. His color was gone, and the life in his face seemed to flicker like a flame running low. He held my hand so tightly. I read the last letter aloud and went to stand— and he gripped my hand even harder and said, "*Don't let me go. If you let me go, I am going to die.*" He said he saw darkness. He said something was in his room—something coming for him, and he began to cry. I wept too and began storming heaven, begging God for a miracle. I opened the Word, tears streaming down my face, desperately searching for some word of hope.

"*Father God, we have come through so much in our lifetime. The enemy of our soul wants nothing more than for us to give up, die, be destroyed. Father, we trust You. We don't know how, but we know you are going to use this. Show us Your fingerprints—Your hand in our lives right now. Amen.*"

I opened my Bible right then to Job Chapter 38. With each verse, I cried...

1 *Then the Lord spoke to Job out of the storm. He said:*

2 *"Who is this that obscures my plans
    with words without knowledge?*
3 *Brace yourself like a man;
    I will question you, and you shall answer me.*
4 *"Where were you when I laid the earth's foundation?
    Tell me, if you understand.*
5 *Who marked off its dimensions? Surely you know!
    Who stretched a measuring line across it?*
6 *On what were its footings set?
    or who laid its cornerstone—*

7 *While the morning stars sang together*
and all the angels[a] shouted for joy?

8 *"Who shut up the sea behind doors*
When it burst forth from the womb,

9 *When I made the clouds its garment*
and wrapped it in thick darkness,

10 *When I fixed limits for it*
and set its doors and bars in place,

11 *When I said, 'This far you may come and no farther;*
here is where your proud waves halt?

12 *"Have you ever given orders to the morning,*
or shown the dawn its place,

13 *that it might take the Earth by the edges*
and shake the wicked out of it?

14 *The earth takes shape like clay under a seal;*
its features stand out like those of a garment.

15 *The wicked are denied their light,*
and their upraised arm is broken.

16 *"Have you journeyed to the springs of the sea*
or walked in the recesses of the deep?

17 *Have the gates of death been shown to you?*
Have you seen the gates of the deepest darkness?

18 *Have you comprehended the vast expanses of the*
earth? Tell me, if you know all this.

19 *"What is the way to the abode of light?*
And where does darkness reside?

20 *Can you take them to their places?*
Do you know the paths to their dwellings?

21 *Surely you know, for you were already born!*
You have lived so many years!

22 *"Have you entered the storehouses of the snow*
or seen the storehouses of the hail,

23 which I reserve for times of trouble,
  for days of war and battle?
24 What is the way to the place where the lightning is
  dispersed? or the place where the east winds are
  scattered over the earth?
25 Who cuts a channel for the torrents of rain,
  and a path for the thunderstorm,
26 to water a land where no one lives,
  an uninhabited desert,
27 to satisfy a desolate wasteland
  and make it sprout with grass?
28 Does the rain have a father?
  Who fathers the drops of dew?
29 From whose womb comes the ice?
  Who gives birth to the frost from the heavens
30 When the waters become hard as stone,
  when the surface of the deep is frozen?
31 "Can you bind the chains[b] of the Pleiades?
  Can you loosen Orion's belt?
32 Can you bring forth the constellations in their
  seasons[c] or lead out the Bear[d] with its cubs?
33 Do you know the laws of the heavens?
  Can you set up God's[e] dominion over the earth?
34 "Can you raise your voice to the clouds
  and cover yourself with a flood of water?
35 Do you send the lightning bolts on their way?
  Do they report to you, 'Here we are'?
36 Who gives the ibis wisdom[f]
  or give the rooster understanding?[g]
37 Who has the wisdom to count the clouds?
  Who can tip over the water jars of the heavens

38 When the dust becomes hard
and the clods of earth stick together?
39 "Do you hunt the prey for the lioness
and satisfy the hunger of the lions
40 When they crouch in their dens
or lie in wait in a thicket?
41 Who provides food for the raven?
When it's young cry out to God
and wander about for lack of food?

This is the picture He paints—His power, His creativity, and His sovereignty. If He set the stars in motion and commanded the morning, will He also be faithful here? Right here in our pain?

I don't know about your faith. You may not share mine, and that's okay. However, I hope you're beginning to understand what the role of faith in God plays within my life. In that *"don't let go of my hand"* moment, I didn't just read about God—I saw Him. I saw His fingerprints on every line of that scripture. He reminded me that He created the earth, separated light from dark, and held back the waves. And if He can do that, surely, He can carry us, too.

A peace filled that room. Not a peace that made sense—but a peace that passed understanding. I heard Him, not audibly, but undeniably: *"I've got this. I've always had you. I've always had Erick. And I always will."*

Here, I unpacked the worry, the need to control, the fear of what's next, and the questions of *"why this"* and *"what now."* It was here that I released the grip I had on how I thought this would all look, and it was here—in that holy surrender—that I sank into His arms and simply trusted Him.

People have asked me, *"How are you not angry with God?"*

I understand the question, but here's the truth: my life has held only a fraction of the suffering that Job endured, and although pain can't be measured or compared, the trials I've walked through have taught me that God doesn't waste suffering. He shows up in it.

I learned a long time ago to play the tape back—to rewind the story of my life and look for the places where God showed up, and I've found Him again and again.

I saw Him in the addiction years—when we lost everything but our family, and somehow rebuilt our lives from the ashes.

I saw Him in 2019 when my son severed an artery carrying a mirror, and God guided my husband's hands to save him.

I saw Him when my 2-year-old granddaughter was attacked by a dog and spared.

I saw Him when another granddaughter stepped into hot coals buried beneath beach sand and was protected.

I saw Him again when our youngest son survived a car crash.

Each time we cried, "*Why, Lord?*"

Each time, it felt like the enemy was coming after our entire family.

Looking back, I trace God's fingerprints through every single one of those moments. We didn't always see Him in the middle, but we can always find Him in the replay.

Things don't always go the way we hope. Life doesn't always play out like we imagine. But God? He is the same. Faithful. Present. Able.

And He will use every broken piece—if we let Him—to write a better story. His story.

We sat in that hospital room and named the miracles. We named the moments. We named the memories.

Healthy. Healing. Here.

On July 5, 2020, Erick completed his seventh surgery. He had just received a blood transfusion. The infections seemed to be under control. It also happened to mark 15 years since he'd been clean and sober.

Someone brought a cake. We shared it with nurses who had become our people. We cried. We smiled. We told the story.

And in that room at Virginia Beach General, I realized that God wasn't just sustaining us—He was writing something new.

He was giving us a new script.

And we weren't letting go of His hand.

And here's what I want you to know:

We don't get to choose our storms, but we do get to choose what we anchor to when they hit.

I've walked through seasons that took the breath out of my lungs—where hope was hanging on by a thread and healing felt like a fairytale. But God never left. Not in the ambulance. Not in the ICU. Not in the surgical waiting room. Not in the middle of my fear. And not in the silence when I begged for a miracle.

If you are in a hospital room of your own—maybe not physically, but emotionally or spiritually—I want to remind you that God still writes new stories. He still shows up. And He still holds your hand.

I never wanted to write this part of the story, but it's also the part where heaven touched earth in the most unexpected ways. Pain turned into purpose. Peace sat in the middle of a storm, and surrender became the doorway to healing.

You don't have to hold it all together. You only need to hold on to God.

Something shifted in my mind during this storm. All my life, I filtered everything through the lens that somehow—somehow—this must have been my fault. I had done something wrong. Maybe I deserved the pain I was walking through. Like I shared before, I believed if I had just done something differently, things would have turned out better. I never got mad at God—not because I was spiritually strong, but because I figured this was just the consequence of my mess.

But this time was different.

There was no way I had caused this. There was no decision I made that brought this on. I wouldn't wish what my husband endured on anyone, and as I sat quietly, hour after hour, pouring out my heart and praying that he would live, and as we read through the book of Job, I began to see something I had missed all along.

I began to play the tape of our lives back. I traced the dots from mess to miracle, from pain to purpose. The moments that once felt like failure, God had used for good. They weren't wasted. They were woven.

Psychologists call this practice *"narrative reframing"*—rewriting your story by identifying redemptive meaning in your past. In faith, we call it testimony. It's Romans 8:28 in action: "*And we know that in all things God works for the good of those who love Him, who have been called according to His purpose.*"

Author and speaker Brené Brown puts it this way: *"Owning our story and loving ourselves through that process is the bravest thing that we'll ever do."*

And I believe God is the one who gives us the courage to do it.

So, I started to see. I started to believe. And I started to surrender—not just my fear, but the false story I had carried for too long. The one that told me everything was my fault. That I was the root of the pain.

In that hospital room, I surrendered that lie, too.

He was giving us a new story. He was giving me a new script.

And now, my go-to question has become: *"Okay, God... how are you going to use this?"*

This thing is touching my life. This thing is touching my family. This thing I didn't expect or ask for—this thing that scares me and that I don't understand. How are You going to use this?

It has completely changed my life. It has brought me into daily conversation with the One who set the stars in the sky, drew the boundaries between dry land and sea, created every living thing, and hung the planets in space. It's how I now approach everything. Every trial. Every unexpected turn. I take my thoughts captive and immediately ask the One who already knew it was coming: *"Okay, God... how will You use this?"*

I may not see it right away, but I can trace His fingerprints all over my story—every page, every paragraph, every period.

📖 Reflection & Renewal: Journal and Action Steps

📃 Scriptures for Meditation:

- *"The Lord is close to the brokenhearted and saves those who are crushed in spirit."* – Psalm 34:18 (NIV)

- *"He gives power to the weak and strength to the powerless."* – Isaiah 40:29 (NLT)

- *"Be still, and know that I am God."* – Psalm 46:10 (NIV)

- *"When you pass through the waters, I will be with you."* – Isaiah 43:2 (NIV)

- *"We are hard pressed on every side, but not crushed; perplexed, but not in despair."* – 2 Corinthians 4:8 (NIV)

- *"Cast all your anxiety on Him because He cares for you."* – 1 Peter 5:7 (NIV)

- *"And we know that in all things God works for the good of those who love Him."* – Romans 8:28 (NIV)

Journal Prompts:

1. What has been your *"don't let go of my hand"* moment? Describe it honestly—emotionally, spiritually, and physically.

2. Where did you see God amid your crisis, or where are you still waiting to see Him?

3. What are you still gripping tightly that you may need to surrender to God?

4. Write out a list of times in your life where you now see His fingerprints—even if you couldn't see them then.

5. If Jesus sat beside you in your hospital room (or during your hardest moment), what do you think He would say to you?

6. What is one step you can take this week to invite God into your healing—mentally, emotionally, or spiritually?

7. What lies about yourself or your past are you ready to release, and what truth will you replace it with?

8. What does "Okay God… how are You going to use this?" look like in your life right now?

✅ Next Steps to Walk Out Healing

- **Pray with brutal honesty.** God can handle your anger, fear, doubt, and heartbreak. Tell Him everything.

- **Start your own "God's Fingerprints" list.** The document answered prayers, divine appointments, or even moments of peace in chaos.

- **Find your people.** Healing requires community. Who are your nurses, your Matts, your prayer warriors? Thank them. Let them walk with you.

- **Saturate your space in worship.** Whether it's music, Scripture, or silence—invite God into the room with you.

- **Name the moments.** Celebrate the victories—big and small. Mark your "clean" dates, your healing anniversaries, your answered prayers.

- **Don't rush the process.** Healing isn't linear. But healing is possible. One surrendered breath at a time.

- **Practice narrative reframing.** Ask yourself how God might be using even this moment to work something good in your life.

📖 Citations, Acknowledgments & Further Study

Key Scripture Reference:

- Book of Job, Chapters 38–39, Holy Bible, New International Version (NIV)
- Romans 8:28, New International Version (NIV)

Quoted Thought Leaders:

- Brené Brown, *The Gifts of Imperfection* (Hazelden, 2010)
- Holy Bible, New International Version (NIV)

Acknowledgments and heartfelt love and admiration:

- To the incredible medical teams at Virginia Beach General and the loving nurses who became family.
- To REACH Orthotics and Matt and Seth—your kindness and hope helped us walk again, literally and spiritually.
- To Hunter and the legal team who stepped in with wisdom, grace, and protection.
- To the countless friends, family, and strangers who blessed us with your prayers, meals, financial gifts, and resources

\

Chapter 6

Writing the New Script

There comes a moment in every healing journey when you realize the old script can't carry you any longer. You've faced addiction and codependency, survived trauma, fought for your marriage, stood in hospital rooms holding hands through suffering, and laid your heaviest burdens before the cross. Chapters 1 through 5 were the unpacking—the raw revealing of everything I had once carried. The chapter where I stood in front of my suitcase, heart wide open. The moment I collapsed in the yard, sobbing. The miracle of recovery. The hospital room where my husband whispered, *"Don't let me go."* These stories were about the tearing down. This chapter is the rebuilding. It's the chapter where I stop living by the script written by pain and start co-writing a new story with the Author of truth, healing, and grace.

You arrive at a crossroads. And at that crossroads, you don't just ask, *"What happened to me?"*—you begin to ask, *"Who am I now?"*

For most of my life, I lived by a script I didn't write. A story shaped by whispers of doubt, shame, and fear—lines I had rehearsed so well, they felt like truth. I believed I wasn't enough, that my mistakes defined me, that if people really knew me, they would turn away. I had to make people like me at any cost. These lies weren't just thoughts; they became the foundation of how I saw myself, how I made choices, and how I moved through the world. And then there were the secrets—ones I held so tightly—convinced that if I let them go, everything would unravel. But the truth is, it was holding onto them that was keeping me sick.

When I realized I had the power to rewrite my story, everything shifted. I didn't have to keep playing the same role, repeating the same painful lines. I could challenge the lies, speak truth over my life, and step into a new narrative—one of healing, freedom, and grace. It wasn't easy. Undoing years of false beliefs felt like tearing down walls brick by brick. With every lie I exposed and every secret I surrendered, weight began to drop from my shoulders. With every conversation with my therapist, every loving word from a friend, and every moment spent in prayer and reading Scripture, I began to feel that weight lifted, not just by my strength, but through the grace of God and the support He placed around me.

This chapter isn't just about letting go of the past—it's about reclaiming the pen and writing a story that reflects who I truly am. A story filled with redemption, self-acceptance, and grace. To help you understand the need for a new script in my mind, I'd like to share some ways the old script was created.

Each year in December, I spend time in reflection on my year. I review my word for the year, my goals, and assess what worked and what didn't. 2022 had been a particularly rough year. My husband suffered a massive stroke in March, altering our lives in ways I could never have imagined. It was one of the hardest years of my life, and that's saying a lot considering the events of 2019 and 2020. By May, I had reached a place where I wasn't sure I could do life anymore the way it was going.

The accident in 2020 had already taken so much from my husband—his sense of taste and smell when that section of his brain was damaged from massive skull fractures, his leg through amputation, and now the stroke had stolen his peripheral vision in both eyes along with his short-term memory. The anxiety and fear were overwhelming for both of us. A dear friend recommended a therapist, and I made the call. I had already seen my doctor and had begun medication to help stabilize my emotions as I worked through our new normal and all that it entailed. Not everyone agrees with medication, but I believe it can be useful, and in my case, it was. For the first time in my life, with meeting my therapist, I had someone to talk to who truly heard me.

My therapist validated my feelings, acknowledging that they were mine, that they were okay to have, and that it was okay to feel them. Validation doesn't mean agreement or enabling—it means listening without judgment, recognizing the legitimacy of the emotion, and offering a safe place for it to land. I remember one particular session where I shared a memory I had long buried—something that had haunted me since childhood. I braced myself for skepticism or dismissal, but instead, he spoke gently and said, *"That must have been incredibly painful."* Just like that, I felt seen. His presence, his tone, and his belief in my experience became a mirror reflecting my worth and my truth—a truth I had nearly forgotten was mine to hold.

There was another time I confessed how deeply I was struggling to cope with the stroke and all that had followed. I was ashamed of my thoughts—ashamed to admit how hard it had been to keep functioning, to keep hoping. I expected judgment. Instead, he sat with me and spoke from his own experience. He spoke out loud the very things I had been too scared to say, too afraid someone would think I was a terrible person or a weak believer. In that sacred space, I realized healing doesn't always come through fixing—it often comes through feeling.

According to psychologist Dr. Marsha Linehan, founder of Dialectical Behavior Therapy (DBT), validation is a critical tool in emotional regulation and recovery, which allows individuals to feel understood and connected rather than dismissed or ignored. Research from the American Psychological Association also highlights that emotional validation helps reduce anxiety, builds trust, and opens the door to deeper healing and change.

It was the first time I had ever stood in the closet of my life, suitcases open, allowing someone else to see everything I had packed away for years. For most of my childhood and early adult life, I was made to feel as though my feelings were wrong. If I expressed hurt, it was dismissed as *"That's not really how you feel,"* or *"No one meant it like that."* If I shared a painful memory, I was told it didn't happen that way or that I was being too sensitive. I learned to question my emotional responses. I began to believe that my internal world was unreliable and flawed. When my therapist said, *"That makes sense,"* or *"I believe you,"* it disarmed decades of doubt. It was the first time I felt heard. Truly heard. Someone understood. Someone stayed. In that space of safety, I could begin to separate my truth from the tangled mess of others' projections. He began to give me assignments, things to watch and read that would have a powerful impact on creating a new narrative.

Words have meaning. You can look them up in a dictionary and see what Webster says they mean, but when people speak them, they carry far more weight than a definition. Tone and inflection, intent and reception—these are the things that give words their lasting power. Belief systems are formed depending on how something is said and how we take it in. Words can affirm, or they can wound. Words can heal, or they can bury us. As Dr. Brene Brown has said, *"Words are maps. They carry our histories, our beliefs, and our perspectives."* The most dangerous lies are often not words spoken by others, but words we begin to whisper to ourselves based on how others' words made us feel.

According to research in the field of Narrative Therapy, the stories we tell ourselves are not only shaped by our experiences but also by the language used to describe them. When we are constantly surrounded by words that belittle, dismiss, or ridicule, we will internalize those narratives. Psychologist Albert Ellis noted that our beliefs—not events—disturb us most. The meaning we attach to words shapes our reality. If a child is told repeatedly, they're *"too sensitive"* or *"making things up,"* it doesn't just sting in the moment—it rewrites how they interpret their entire emotional world. And if that's the script you're handed early in life, it takes incredible courage to tear it up and write a new one.

For example, when you were upset, you might have been told, *"Stop crying, you're being dramatic"*. The intent may have been to get you to calm down, but the effect is often silencing. Or maybe someone laughed when you shared a serious thought, and that moment stayed with you, teaching you to withhold in the future. Even compliments can be twisted into pressure: *"You're so strong"* can feel like you're not allowed to show weakness. These moments pile up, layer after layer, until you don't trust your voice or emotions.

Words spoken to and about me—even words spoken to others around me—shaped the script inside my head. When others were praised for certain traits I didn't have, or were encouraged while I was criticized, it wasn't just about comparison. It was a slow and silent schooling in shame. Even as I watched other children in the same family or classroom be told they were "*so sweet*" or "*so tiny*," I heard different messages—warnings about food, being watched closely, or being singled out for correction. Those weren't just isolated comments; they were patterns. They made me feel like I had to earn approval, shrink myself, and strive harder just to be acceptable. Even when the words weren't directed at me, I internalized them. I learned what was celebrated and tolerated— areas where I seemed to fall short. Over time, those unspoken lessons—those messages wrapped in tone, inflection, body language, and glances—became beliefs that echoed within me long after the voices had gone quiet.

I still battle with those voices. They don't go away entirely, but now, I have a process—a spiritual and mental muscle memory—that helps me confront them. I take my thoughts captive, as 2 Corinthians 10:5 teaches, "*and we take captive every thought to make it obedient to Christ.*" This means I actively examine the narrative running through my mind. Is this thought true? Is it rooted in love or fear? Does it align with who God says I am? Cognitive-behavioral therapy (CBT) echoes this process, teaching that distorted thinking patterns can be interrupted and replaced with healthier, truthful responses. When a thought arises that tries to pull me back into shame, I name it, challenge it, and replace it with truth. It's not about pretending the pain never happened—it's about choosing not to let it define me anymore.

With weekly therapy, I was working through some pretty heavy stuff, unpacking a lot of junk—junk that no longer fit, much like my clothes at the time. I was the heaviest I had ever been physically, mentally, and emotionally. Remember the old commercial where the guy said, "*I pick things up and put them down*"? That was me. I would unpack some lies, replace them with truths, but still hold on to the dark parts that kept me hiding behind my weight. Everyone was comfortable with that version of me—it seemed easier for them if I stayed in the familiar heartache I had always known. Maybe that was perceived - maybe the script my mind played. I would ask God for healing in these areas, then something would happen—a memory would be triggered by a familiar sight, sound, or smell, and everything would come rushing back. I wanted healing so badly. I wanted to be free.

I had been the victim of sexual abuse. I had endured verbal, mental, and emotional abuse that chipped away at my sense of self, at my ability to trust, at my belief that I was worthy of love without conditions. These wounds ran deep, forming the foundation of the script I carried—the one that told me I was never enough, never worthy, never quite right. The pain from these experiences settled into my bones, shaping how I viewed myself and the world around me. It became the lens through which I saw every interaction, every relationship, every challenge.

Then there were family gatherings and get-togethers where it seemed that bringing up embarrassing moments along with your shortcomings got the most laughs. Maybe it made some people feel relevant, or thought it was funny, but for me, it drove me deeper into myself. The judgment I felt at times was overwhelming. As I worked through therapy, I realized that I had a voice. I shared with my therapist how I felt when people brought up embarrassing things about me or called out my mistakes or shortcomings as if they were a joke—food for laughter. I shared how it would cause me to withdraw and dread being in certain situations, and that it had spilled over into my daily life. Into my work. Imposter syndrome became a real thing. I was worried that I would start talking or sharing, and someone would laugh, call me out, tell the room I was wrong, point out and make a public spectacle of my shortcomings, and I would lose my voice, standing there with tears, unable to breathe or move. I played that script over and over in my mind.

We talked through my successes. That I had just been in the top 500 Realtors in my area, when, at that time, there were over 10,000. My therapist asked me, *"How could someone who doesn't know what they're doing accomplish that?"* He reminded me of the clients who had trusted me, the referrals I'd received, and the people who believed in me. Together, we journaled through it all, making lists of my strengths and weaknesses, setting plans to improve the weak spots, and further develop the strong ones. We were tackling, naming, and rewriting one lie and limiting belief at a time.

Maybe you've felt that too—like laughter wasn't lighthearted but laced with judgment. Maybe, you've sat silently, like I did, pretending to smile while something inside you folded in on itself. If you have, I want you to know you're not alone. You are not what they say about you. You are not the sum of your most embarrassing moments. And you do not have to live by a script someone else wrote in sarcasm.

That's the danger of unchecked shame. Left alone, it writes the whole story. But not anymore. Not for me. Not for you. I'm done letting the echoes of someone else's laughter define who I am. I'm not perfect. I'm learning to speak up, rewrite, and reclaim.

According to Dr. Kristin Neff, self-compassion researcher and author, a huge part of healing from impostor syndrome and shame-based thinking is being honest about our pain without judgment. Self-compassion means treating yourself with the same kindness and care that you would offer a close friend. Studies show that self-compassion can lead to greater resilience, motivation, and emotional well-being (Neff, 2003). As I rewrote my script, I realized that grace isn't just something we offer others—it's something we must extend to ourselves, too.

If someone you love is experiencing what I described, or if you, yourself, have been stuck in that loop of silence and shame, know this: Your voice is not too broken to be heard. Your story is not too messy to be rewritten. You're not alone—and you never were.

Then it started being about others' shortcomings, mistakes, and failures. It became jabs and jeers about others. It became people using names as if they were bad words. I sat there and realized I had silenced myself and was now watching the same thing happen to others I love. We talked about how, for many years, I sat in silence when I should have spoken up. How I beat myself up for the lessons I must have taught my kids on keeping quiet, and how others can walk on them, use them, and scapegoat them. I did a lot of beating myself up, because the script in my head made me believe someone else's happiness or comfort was more important than mine. I couldn't have something just for me. I had to share it, give it away, justify why it should be mine. I couldn't speak up and stand up for myself or others.

As I wrestled through this, I returned to the story in the Bible from John 8:3–11. Jesus is teaching in the temple when the Pharisees bring in a woman caught in adultery. They accuse her and demand that she be stoned. But Jesus, instead of condemning her, bends down and writes in the dust. Then He says, *"Let the one who has never sinned throw the first stone."* One by one, the accusers drop their stones and walk away. Then Jesus, the only one truly without sin, looks at her and says, *"Neither do I condemn you. Go now and leave your life of sin."*

That story has stayed with me. I sent a message to my family just before Easter that year, asking that our home become a safe place.

When we gathered, we left outside the door the need to bring up someone else's past, make jokes at another's expense, or talk about people who aren't in the room. I'm so glad I haven't been stoned for my past. I am freely forgiven. In any room, at any given time, if a screen hovered above our heads showing every fault, many who once stood tall would be silent. They are the ones who, like those accusers in John 8, would drop their stones and walk away.

We don't know what Jesus wrote in the sand that day, but we do know what He offered: mercy, dignity, and grace. I am like that woman—and like the woman at the well—am fully known and fully loved by God. We all are. There will always be something we could have done differently—some regret we wish we could erase. But we can choose to stop throwing stones at ourselves and each other. We can write a new script. One grounded not in shame and silence, but in truth and compassion.

Psychologists suggest that people often resort to sarcasm or joking at others' expense as a way of deflecting from their own insecurities or avoiding their own emotional vulnerabilities (Holmgren & Eisenberg, 2021). Recognizing this doesn't excuse the behavior, but it can help us understand the root cause. With awareness, we can change. We can speak up with courage and kindness. We can set boundaries. And we can lead by example—creating safe spaces, rewriting toxic scripts, and walking in the grace so freely given to us.

According to Brené Brown, *"Shame needs three things to grow: secrecy, silence, and judgment."* But healing? Healing needs safety, compassion, and truth. We get to decide which environment we'll nurture—first for ourselves, and then for others.

Rewriting the Script: Real-Life Practices

By now, you may be wondering: What does rewriting the script actually look like in daily life? For me, it wasn't one big dramatic moment. It was a hundred small decisions that began to shift the narrative.

- **Taking thoughts captive** (2 Corinthians 10:5). This looked like recognizing when shame tried to creep in—when I'd think, *"You always mess this up,"* I'd stop and replace it with, *"You're learning, and growth takes time."* I began to speak the truth out loud.
- **Setting boundaries**—with family, with work, with conversations. Boundaries are not ultimatums. They're fences—healthy structures that protect our emotional, physical, and spiritual well-being. As Dr. Henry Cloud and Dr. John Townsend describe in *Boundaries* (1992), boundaries help us define what is ours to own and what is not. They allow us to say yes and no with clarity and love, and they preserve our peace without punishing others.
- **Daily journaling and Scripture reading**—writing down my fears, then finding the truth to counteract them.
- **Celebrating wins, no matter how small**—because shame thrives in silence, but freedom thrives in celebration.
- **Therapy and community**—inviting others to speak life over the dark places and not isolating when the old voices get loud.

Rewriting the script didn't mean pretending the past never happened. It meant looking it in the eye and saying, *"You don't get to control me anymore."*

Understanding Perfectionism

The next rewrite of my script deals with perfectionism. We've discussed this in previous chapters, but it bears repeating—especially here. People who've experienced emotional, mental, or physical abuse often process their pain through perfectionism. It becomes their armor. If everything looks good on the outside, maybe they can keep the chaos on the inside from spilling out.

According to researcher and author Brené Brown, perfectionism isn't about self-improvement; it's about trying to earn approval and avoid shame. It's the belief that, if I look perfect, I will live and work perfectly. I will avoid or minimize the painful feelings of blame, judgment, and shame (Brown, 2010).

This belief system creates unrealistic expectations not just for ourselves but for those around us. We can begin to hold others to the same impossible standards we have for ourselves, which can deeply impact our relationships.

I recognized this in myself and worked intentionally to let go of perfectionism. It meant being okay with *"good enough,"* allowing room for grace, and remembering that progress is still progress—even if it's messy. I started to extend the same compassion to myself that I offered others, and slowly, the weight of having to *"get it all right"* began to lift.

I struggled with things not being good enough. The messages I received told me there was a better way to do it, and that my best wasn't good enough. I remember one day when my kids were folding towels in the linen closet, I caught myself criticizing how they had folded them. At that moment, I realized I was doing the very thing I hated—the thing that had shaped me in so many painful ways. I stopped, looked at my girls crying, and apologized. They were just towels. In a closet, nonetheless. The lie that everything had to be perfect, that no one could see "*things*" out of place, had come from stuffing conditions into my suitcase—conditions placed on validation, acceptance, and love. More lies that I had carried like an anvil in my bag.

I'm dumping perfectionism out of my suitcase, and I made a vow to God not to repack it. I want Him to reshape my view on perfectionism and redefine how I see worth, value, and effort—not through the lens of performance, but through His eyes of grace. I want Him to write the script of my minutes, hours, days, weeks, and years.

Scripture speaks directly to this:

- *"Whatever you do, work heartily, as for the Lord and not for men."* — Colossians 3:23 (ESV)
- *"But he said to me, 'My grace is sufficient for you, for my power is made perfect in weakness.'"* — 2 Corinthians 12:9 (NIV)
- *"The Lord your God is with you, the Mighty Warrior who saves. He will take great delight in you; in His love He will no longer rebuke you, but will rejoice over you with singing."* — Zephaniah 3:17 (NIV)

These verses remind me that God isn't expecting perfection—He's looking for surrender, obedience, and trust. He knows the intentions of my heart and honors every step toward growth, no matter how small.

I had plenty of work to do. I had things to surrender, cut off, and lay to rest. I had some decisions to make.

There comes a time when you get sick and tired of being sick and tired. That's where I was. I didn't want to keep reacting out of pain, trauma, or old programming. My word for the year was reset. I wasn't just resetting my calendar—I was resetting me—my mindset, my emotional reflexes, and my spiritual posture. I was done shrinking, done second-guessing, and done apologizing for taking up space in a world I was born to impact.

I had lived so long thinking everything was my fault. Someone was upset? Must've been me. Something fell apart? Must've been my failure. I played the tape backwards so often I practically wore it out—rehashing every mistake, and every word I wished I could take back. But I finally realized: I needed a new default setting. Just as your dryer has a default, or your GPS reroutes when you miss a turn, I needed to hardwire in a different emotional response. One rooted in truth, grace, and growth.

Now hear me clearly: there is no magic switch. Growth is a process. And sometimes it ain't pretty. I began asking myself, what if I don't default to defense? What if I don't immediately assume I'm the problem? What if I paused long enough to ask, *"Is this true? Is this mine to carry?"* What if I actually believed that true healing was possible?

And you know what I found? It is possible. But it's not a one-time thing. It's the slow, steady drip of intentional choices. You don't cut out a canyon with one drop of water—you get it from millions of drops over time, carving away the hard edges. That's how transformation happens, too. Not in the flashy moments, but in the faithful ones. The ones where you show up for yourself, even when it's hard. Especially when it's hard.

This chapter of my life was about permitting myself to feel, to process, and to grow. As Lysa TerKeurst says, *"Feel it. Own it. But don't live there."* Period. There are no ifs, ands, or buts. You are entitled to your feelings. What you're not obligated to do is stay stuck in them. You get to move forward.

Growth meant owning the parts of the process I had tried to ignore. Yes, life had dealt me some awful cards—but that didn't mean I had to keep playing a losing hand. I chose to lay down bitterness and pick up better. I chose to stop blaming the storm and start becoming the anchor.

Life will still throw curveballs. People will still talk, but I've learned that my peace is non-negotiable, and my healing is holy work.

Flipping the Script on Food & Body Image

If I'm being honest, I've wrestled with my weight for most of my life. Not just the number on the scale, but the meaning behind it. The shame. The fear. The judgment—both from others and from myself. For a long time, I believed exactly what the world told me: my weight issues were because I was lazy, undisciplined, or just not trying hard enough.

But let's set the record straight—weight struggles are not always about willpower.

Over these last two years, I've learned something crucial: food is often a symptom, not the root issue. It's a comforter, a reward, a punishment, a coping mechanism. We eat to celebrate. We eat to mourn. We eat because we're stressed, lonely, anxious, or just trying to survive one more hard moment.

I had to confront the truth that my relationship with food was shaped by much more than cravings. I had to go back—way back—and start telling myself a different story. With the help of my therapist, I began peeling back the layers. We talked through trauma, self-worth, body image, and all the lies I'd believed about myself and my body. And let me tell you—those conversations were heavy. But they were also holy.

It's no wonder so many of us are hurting in silence. Society praises thinness like a badge of honor, but shames the people who need compassion most. Diet culture has made billions convincing people that a smaller body equals a better life, but here's the truth: you can't hate yourself into health.

Dr. Anita Johnston writes in her book, *Eating in the Light of the Moon*, *"Eating disorders are not about food. They are about our hunger for something deeper—connection, belonging, understanding."* And isn't that true? Sometimes, what we really hunger for has nothing to do with food.

I've battled an unhealthy body image, food fears, and the deep-rooted belief that I had to earn love by shrinking myself. If I could look a certain way, I would finally be enough for the world.

But the truth is, I was always enough. I didn't believe it yet.

And so, I started flipping the script.

I began choosing foods that nourished me instead of numbing me. I stopped labeling foods as *"good"* or *"bad"* and started asking, *"How does this make me feel?"* I traded guilt for curiosity. I leaned into movement that felt joyful, not punishing. I learned that self-discipline and self-compassion are not enemies—they're partners.

I'm still on the journey. Some days are hard. Some meals are messy, but I'm not chasing skinny anymore. I'm chasing freedom.

If you've ever felt trapped in your own body or ashamed of your reflection, I want you to hear this: You are not your weight. You are not your worst day. You are not a failure because you struggle.

And if no one's told you today, let me be the one—you are worth the work of healing.

To understand the depth of the reset I needed, I have to go back— way back—to the moments that shaped how I saw myself and how I believed the world saw me, too.

I remember avoiding PE class—not because I didn't want to move, but because I couldn't bear to be watched. I couldn't handle the stares, the comments, the snickers. So, I took the failing grade and made it up in Health class. That, to me, felt like survival. Because being seen meant being judged. Being laughed at. Being measured and found wanting.

During sixth grade, my parents wanted to help me become healthier. Their hearts were in the right place—they loved and wanted the best for me, but sometimes even well-meant efforts can leave unintended scars.

My dad started taking me jogging with him. I know now it was his way of trying to spend time with me and encourage me, but at the time, all I felt was the burning sting of humiliation. The tears would start—quietly at first, then flood my face—as we jogged past houses of classmates who later would say cruel things. The names. The laughter. The jeers.

I didn't hate my dad for trying. I hated how it made me feel—small, exposed, and ashamed. I hated jogging. I hated the calisthenics at each corner. More than anything else, I hated feeling like I was failing at something that was supposed to help me.

I didn't get any stronger from jogging. I didn't get more motivated. I only got smaller on the inside. I shrank into myself and started believing that I was the problem. My body was the reason I wasn't enough.

Every time someone else was called so pretty, so tiny, such a cutie, it carved that message a little deeper. I wasn't the pretty one. I wasn't the little one. I was the girl who had to skip the treat, who had to run the block, who was always too much of something—too big, too slow, too different.

I remember beginning to sneak food. Not because I didn't know better, but because it had become this symbol of shame and scarcity. When food is withheld—when it's used as punishment or control—it becomes something you crave not just with your stomach, but with your soul. That's how disordered eating begins. That's how shame grows.

And let's call it what it is: eating disorders don't always look like the textbook. Sometimes it's not binging or starving. Sometimes it's the constant mental math, the guilt after eating something "*bad,*" the anxiety about being seen while eating in public. It's the inner critic that never shuts up. It's the deep belief that your body is a burden.

And those messages? They don't come out of nowhere.

We speak life or death over children with our words. Especially in the 1980s—back when we said things like "*big-boned,*" "*husky,*" "*thick,*" "*chunky,*" and "*awkward*" like it was just part of growing up. We praised the cute and the skinny kids and the tall and the athletic ones like they had earned something holy. We didn't realize that the kids, hearing what they weren't, were building their identity around that absence.

We teach our children, without even realizing it, that their value is tied to how they look, not who they are.

And those words—they stick. They form the internal soundtrack that plays for decades unless we stop the music and reset the station.

That's why this chapter of my life matters so much. I've been rewinding the old tapes. I've been learning to speak life over myself. To reclaim joy in movement. To see food as fuel, not as the enemy. To find my voice in a culture that told me to sit quietly and try to take up less space.

So, if you've ever carried those same wounds... if you're still fighting the echoes of words spoken over your younger self... please hear me:

You are not what they said.
You are not the weight you carry.
You are not too much.
You are enough.

Let's keep going.

The battle began—the twisted, tangled war of don't eat, but eat.

Don't eat, because thinner means worthy. But eat, because if you stay heavy, maybe they'll leave you alone. Maybe you won't be a target. Maybe if you hide behind enough layers—of weight, of clothes, of silence—they won't see you. And if they do? Well, then maybe... maybe they actually care. Maybe they really like me.

It's a cruel contradiction, and it's the kind of mental prison that abuse creates. You stop trusting your body. You stop trusting food.

You stop trusting yourself, because the trauma rewrites everything—especially your relationship with safety.

When you've experienced emotional, mental, or sexual abuse, food becomes a weapon and a shield. Control becomes your survival strategy. You eat to cope, to punish, to comfort, to disappear. And every time you try to break free, that voice sneaks in again, whispering, *"What if it happens again? What if they see you? What if they want you?"*

So, you stay hidden even if it means staying hurt.

And that's the vicious cycle—you mask behind the very thing you hate. You carry the weight to feel safe, but then hate yourself for it. You want to be seen, but you're terrified of being visible. You long for love, but you don't believe you deserve it unless you're smaller, quieter, less. So, you swing between restriction and rebellion, shame and starvation, hoping somehow it all makes sense.

It doesn't. It won't. Because the truth is: the abuse wasn't your fault. The trauma was never yours to carry. But the healing? That's your right to claim.

I had to stop using my body as a battleground. I had to stop punishing myself for someone else's sins. The weight, the struggle, the pain—it was all trying to protect me. But I didn't need protection anymore. I needed peace.

Peace came when I stopped hiding. When I stopped shrinking. When I stood in the mirror and said, *"You are not broken. You are not the abuse. You are not too much. You are not too big. You are not invisible. You are seen, known, and deeply loved."*

And just when I thought I had to carry it alone, something broke open.

My husband—this man who saw me through the years—through the struggles and the silence—would look at me and say, *"You're beautiful."* He told me he wanted me, desired me. But I couldn't believe him. I wouldn't believe him. I thought he must be lying. How could he want this woman? How could he see me—really see me—and still want to stay?

It all came crashing down one afternoon after therapy. Something in me couldn't hold it back anymore. I poured it out, every bit of it. The shame. The years of hiding. The reasons behind my body image, my fear, my eating patterns, and my silence. I told him why I couldn't believe I was beautiful. I told him why I flinched when he touched me, why I kept the lights off, and why I couldn't stand my reflection in the mirror. My voice was shaking. My face was soaked with tears. And I was certain—this is where he walks away.

But he didn't.

He didn't flinch. He didn't look away. He didn't interrupt or minimize it or try to fix it. He just stayed. He listened to the parts of my story I had never spoken aloud. And instead of turning away, he leaned in.

He told me he loved me—not the version of me I was trying to become, but the real me—the person sitting across from him in that raw, broken, tear-streaked moment. The me I thought was too far gone to be cherished.

And that changed something.

Because love—the real kind—isn't based on dress sizes, perfect skin, or how *"put together"* you look. It's not earned through performance, weight loss, or shrinking yourself to fit someone else's fantasy.

Real love stays.
Real love sees.
Real love heals.

That day, I learned I didn't have to measure up to be worth loving. I already was.

Even as I type these words, the tears stream down my face.

Not because I'm still broken.
Not because I'm ashamed.
But because I'm still healing. And this part of my journey... It's far from over.

There are days I still look in the mirror and have to choose truth over lies. There are moments when food still whispers old comforts, and shame tries to wrap itself around me like a blanket. There are echoes of old pain, and yes, sometimes they get loud. But I've learned to talk back now. I've learned to stand in that pain and not let it take the pen from my hand.

Because I'm the one writing this story.
Not my past. Not my trauma. Not the scale.
Me.

And if you're still walking this road too—if your journey with your body, your worth, your voice, or your healing, still feels messy—I want you to know: you're not behind. You're becoming.

You are not the girl who was teased, or the woman who hid, or the one who thought she had to earn love.
You are more.
You are becoming.
And even in the tears... You are healing.

📖 Reflection & Renewal: Journal and Action Steps

📃 Scriptures for Meditation:

- **2 Corinthians 10:5 (ESV):** *"We take captive every thought to make it obedient to Christ."*

- **Romans 12:2 (NIV):** *"Do not conform to the pattern of this world, but be transformed by the renewing of your mind."*

- **Psalm 34:18 (NIV):** *"The Lord is close to the brokenhearted and saves those who are crushed in spirit."*

- **Isaiah 61:3 (NLT):** *"...to bestow on them a crown of beauty instead of ashes, the oil of joy instead of mourning..."*

- **Zephaniah 3:17 (NIV):** *"He will take great delight in you... He will rejoice over you with singing."*

✎ Journal Prompts:

1. What was the old script I've lived by? What words or beliefs shaped it?

2. What messages did I receive during childhood that echo in how I view myself today?

3. Where have I seen shame disguised as love or concern? How did it affect my body image and worth?

4. How has trauma shaped my relationship with food, my body, and control?

5. In what ways have I masked pain through perfectionism or silence?

6. Who has seen me at my lowest and stayed? What did that teach me about love?

7. What truth do I want to begin speaking over my body, my mind, and my story from this day forward?

✅ Next Steps to Walk Out Healing:

- **Speak your truth out loud.** Share your story—whether with a therapist, loved one, or trusted circle. Shame shrinks in the presence of safety.

- **Write your affirmations in your own handwriting.** Keep them visible. Begin with: *"I am loved. I am healing. I am not my past. I am writing a new story."*

- **Reclaim sacred movement.** Choose one joyful way to move your body this week that honors—not punishes—you.
- **Revisit the Word daily.** Let Scripture be your soundtrack, not the lies of your past.

- **Celebrate healing, even if it's slow.** Create a *"progress jar"* and note even the smallest moments of growth.

Citations, Acknowledgments & Further Study:

- **Dr. Marsha Linehan** – Creator of Dialectical Behavior Therapy (DBT); noted for her work in validation and emotional regulation.

- **Dr. Anita Johnston** – *Eating in the Light of the Moon*; explores the emotional roots of eating disorders and disordered eating patterns.

- **Dr. Kristin Neff** – Leading self-compassion researcher; author of *Self-Compassion: The Proven Power of Being Kind to Yourself.*

- **Dr. Brené Brown** – *The Gifts of Imperfection and Daring Greatly*; expert on shame, vulnerability, and wholehearted living.

- **Drs. Henry Cloud & John Townsend** – Boundaries; foundational work on emotional health and setting protective limits.

- **Albert Ellis** – Founder of Rational Emotive Behavior Therapy (REBT); emphasized that it's our beliefs about events—not the events themselves—that cause distress.

- **American Psychological Association** – Research on trauma, narrative therapy, and the impact of validation on healing.

- **Holy Bible (NIV, ESV, NLT)** – Source for all cited scriptures.

Chapter 7

Thriving

Seeding the Clouds

Before discussing what it means to thrive, I should acknowledge the road traveled to get here.

The earlier chapters of my story—those pages were heavy. They were filled with unpacking trauma, peeling back shame, and finding my voice after years of silence. I wrote about addiction and codependency, about emotional, mental, and sexual abuse. I shared what it felt like to lose my footing, to carry burdens not meant for me, and to heal in the arms of grace. I stood face-to-face with perfectionism, broken by shame, and challenged the lies that shaped my self-worth.

I faced the mirror and confronted the stories I'd spent decades believing—that I was too much and not enough at the same time. That I had to earn love. That my voice didn't matter. That healing was for other people.

But I also discovered the truth.

I learned that I am not my past.

That I am not my weight.
That the love of my husband wasn't conditional—it was covenant.
That God doesn't look at the surface—He looks at the heart.
That healing doesn't happen in hiding—it happens in honesty.
That grace isn't just something we offer others—it's something we must learn to extend to ourselves.

And now, standing on the other side of that mountain of unpacking, I see something new in the distance: growth.

The pain didn't disappear, but it stopped writing the script. With that, I picked up the pen and started writing a new one—one of freedom, fullness, and forward motion. A story not just of survival, but of revival.

On January 1, 2024, I woke up and made a new declaration: I am learning to seed the clouds.

Cloud seeding is a real process in the natural world. It's when a substance is introduced into the sky to change what comes from it, usually to produce rain or snow. In my life, cloud seeding became a metaphor for something deeper. It meant intentionally investing in the atmosphere I wanted to live in. It meant believing that what I sowed today would change what fell tomorrow.

I wasn't wishing anymore. I was planting.
I wasn't bracing for the next storm. I was expecting rain.
I had lived long enough in drought—spiritually, mentally, emotionally, and physically.
Now, it was time to thrive.

What Does It Mean to Thrive?

According to the dictionary, *"thrive"* means *"to grow vigorously; to flourish, to progress toward or realize a goal despite or because of circumstances."*

But when you've lived through trauma, addiction, abuse, neglect, or abandonment, thriving doesn't always feel like an option. It feels like a luxury word. A word for other people. A word for the healed, the strong, the ones who didn't carry the baggage you carried.

Let me be clear: thriving is not reserved for the perfect. Thriving is a birthright for the broken. I am made to thrive. You are made to thrive.

Spiritually, to thrive means to live connected to the Source of all life—God Himself. It's not about pretending you're okay. It's not about functioning. It's not about doing what makes everyone else comfortable because, as long as you stay stuck, they don't have to face the fact that they may need to change. It's about being rooted in truth, even when the world around you is shaking. It's choosing to grow in the hard soil. It's rising, not because life is easy, but because grace is real.

In clinical recovery, thriving is when a person moves beyond survival. It's when we begin to form safe attachments, regulate our emotions, build new neural pathways, reclaim our agency, and pursue a life that isn't built on reaction but on renewal. It means your story is no longer defined by what happened to you, but by what you now choose to build from it.

I know this road because I am walking it right now, in real time—right now, as I am writing this book—right now, as you are reading this book—and forever.

🌱 Thriving Mentally – Rewriting the Narrative

Definition: To thrive mentally is cultivating a renewed, stable, and empowered mind, not free from struggle, but full of tools, truth, and authority over the script that plays in your head.

Spiritually: Romans 12:2 reminds us, "*Be transformed by the renewing of your mind.*" This is not a one-time change—it's the daily act of letting God rewrite what shame and fear once wrote. It's the hard, holy work of choosing truth over trauma, grace over guilt, and peace over panic.

Clinically:
In trauma-informed recovery, we learn that the mind absorbs patterns of thought like scars. A scarcity mindset—believing there's not enough love, time, worth, or safety—keeps us in survival mode, and when you've endured emotional or physical trauma, it's common to develop a belief that everything is your fault—even when you're suffering from someone else's consequences. This "*toxic responsibility*" mindset forms early and hardens over time... until we learn to interrupt it with truth.

My Story:
I used to live in a perpetual state of blame and lack. If something went wrong, it must've been my fault. If someone was upset, I assumed I had caused it. If I was suffering, it was somehow what I deserved.

That mindset? It'll keep you stuck. It'll keep you silent. It'll have you apologizing for taking up space, for having needs, or even existing. And I carried that into everything—my work, parenting, and marriage. I'd over-function, over-apologize, and under-value myself. In moments when I was affected by someone else's choices, I still believed I was the one to fix it, cover it, or pay the price.

But not anymore.
Now I ask, *"Is this mine to carry?"*
Now I pause and pray before I spiral.
Now I speak the truth over triggers.
Now I permit myself to rewrite the lies that were planted in fear.

Action Steps:

- **Identify the Lie.** When something goes wrong, stop and ask, *"Is this really mine to own?"*
- **Replace Scarcity with Truth.** Write down God's promises of abundance: love, grace, strength, peace—they are not in short supply.
- **Reframe Fault into Focus.** Shift from *"What did I do wrong?"* to *"What am I learning? What does healing require right now?"*
- **Practice the Pause.** Before rushing to fix, pause. Breathe. Invite God into the space where you used to insert blame.
- **Create a *"Not Mine"* List.** Write down things that are not your responsibility and pray over them as you release them.

Thriving Physically – Honoring the Body You're In

Definition: To thrive physically is to care for your body not from a place of punishment, but from a place of purpose. Choose movement, nourishment, rest, and rhythm that align with love—not shame.

Spiritually: *"Do you not know that your bodies are temples of the Holy Spirit...? Therefore, honor God with your bodies."* — 1 Corinthians 6:19–20 (NIV)

For too long, I viewed my body as the enemy. A thing to be fought. Fixed. Hidden. Silenced. But God doesn't see it that way. He created this body, not as a burden, but as a vessel of glory. Thriving physically isn't about chasing a number. It's about partnering with the body God gave me and treating it with honor, care, and compassion.

Clinically:

For survivors of abuse and neglect, the body often becomes a place of trauma. Dissociation, body dysmorphia, and chronic fatigue can all be linked to early messages of shame. Thriving physically doesn't start with a gym membership—it begins with reconnecting to your physical presence. Trauma-sensitive movement, somatic healing practices, and gentle consistency are all steps forward.

My Story:

There was a season when I hated my body. I really hated it. I hid from mirrors. I layered clothes. I apologized for my shape, my presence, even my needs. I punished my body with restriction or over-exercise and used food to numb what I couldn't name. As healing took root, I stopped seeing my body as the battleground and started treating it like an ally. I stopped asking, *"How do I look?"* and started asking, *"How do I feel?"*

I don't exercise to erase myself—I move to honor my journey. I don't eat to shame or soothe—I eat to nourish and fuel. And when I rest? I rest like it's sacred. Because it is. I am learning not to fear food.

Action Steps:

- **Daily Movement**: Choose something gentle but consistent. Walk. Stretch. Dance. Celebrate what your body can do.

- **Nourish with Intention**: Focus on adding foods that give you life, not restricting out of fear. Ask, *"How will this make me feel after I eat it?"* I have had to add *"Why am I eating it?"* The pattern of masking emotions behind food and feeling something else is real. I have to fight against it.
- **Practice Breathing.** It probably sounds silly, but I regularly found myself holding my breath, with my shoulders up, and my jaw clenched. Learning to breathe and release stress has been another way I am learning to help rewrite my script and thrive.
- **Rest on Purpose**: Schedule rest like it matters—because it does. Sleep, unplugging, Sabbath.
- **Body Gratitude List**: Each week, write down 3 things your body did for you. Not how it looks, but what it accomplished.
- **It's not about a number:** I will go weeks now without looking at the scale. That is not what it is about for me. I don't want to get hung up on the same old things. I want a new mindset and a new life.

💜 Thriving Emotionally – Healing the Hidden Parts

Definition: To thrive emotionally is to feel fully and freely without being ruled by emotion or numbing it into silence. It's the sacred practice of honoring what you feel, processing it with truth, and not letting it define your worth or decisions. It is knowing and declaring, *"I have a right to feel exactly what I am feeling."* No permission is needed. It isn't about assigning, rather it's right or wrong.

Spiritually: *"The Lord is close to the brokenhearted and saves those who are crushed in spirit."* — Psalm 34:18 (NIV)
Thriving emotionally doesn't mean we won't cry. It means we won't

drown. It means we can allow ourselves to feel deeply when we are anchored in God's truth. Scripture displays again, and again—David wept, Jesus wept, Elijah wanted to give up under a tree. Emotions are not sin. They're signals. When we bring them to God instead of burying them, He will meet us right there in the middle.

Clinically:

Emotionally thriving means learning to regulate—not repress. It involves building what trauma therapists call *"emotional tolerance"*—the ability to experience strong feelings without being overwhelmed by them or driven to destructive coping mechanisms. (It's that reset I have talked about throughout this book. Creating a new default so you can feel without starting the old reel-to-reel playing.) According to DBT (Dialectical Behavior Therapy), skills such as distress tolerance, mindfulness, and emotional validation are essential for moving from chaos to calm. Healing emotionally often requires revisiting core wounds and reparenting ourselves with gentleness, boundaries, and voice.

My Story:

For most of my life, I didn't know how to trust my emotions. I had been told they were *"too much,"* *"too dramatic,"* or *"not real."* So, I learned to silence them, to stuff them down, and smile through the pain.

But silence doesn't heal—it hardens. And when I finally sat in therapy and let the tears come, I felt like a dam broke. There were years of grief, anger, fear, and shame behind that wall.

One of the hardest things I needed to learn was that I am allowed to feel.

I can cry without apologizing.
I can be angry without exploding.

I can grieve without losing my faith.

I can feel joy without waiting for the other shoe to drop.

Emotional thriving isn't about continuously feeling happy. it's about feeling everything with integrity. It's about no longer editing your emotions to make others more comfortable. It's about finally being safe with yourself.

I had a session with my therapist that I'll never forget. He asked me to write a list of things I liked—my favorite foods, places to go, activities I enjoy, books, movies, songs... And I sat there, staring at the page. Frozen. Blank.

You would think this would be the easiest list to make, but it was one of the hardest things I've ever done.

Why? Because when you've spent your life trying to keep everyone else happy, safe, and okay... You lose sight of what you enjoy. You become so conditioned to adapt—anticipating someone else's preferences, moods, and needs—that your voice gets lost in the noise. And somewhere along the line, you stop asking, "What do I want?" because the answer feels foreign... or selfish... or simply unknown.

That blank page revealed a painful truth: I had never fully learned how to hold space for myself.

This happens to so many of us who've lived under chronic stress, abuse, or emotional neglect. Especially as women, we're often taught to serve, sacrifice, say yes, and to keep the peace. Doing that long enough, we become experts in everyone else's lives—but strangers in our own.

Writing that list felt like meeting myself for the first time. At first, it felt awkward, but over time, I began to rediscover what made me feel joy—not to please others, but to reconnect with who God created me to be.

Action Steps:

- **Name Your Emotions**: Give your feelings language. Say out loud, *"I feel _____ because _____."* Naming reduces shame.
- **Validate and Respond, Don't React**: Use DBT's core skill— pause, breathe, validate, then choose a response.
- **Daily Emotional Check-Ins**: Ask, *"What am I feeling right now?"* and *"What do I need right now?"*
- **Safe Expression Practices**: Journal, speak to a trusted friend or therapist, cry, or scream into a pillow—move the emotion through, not around.
- **Reparenting Rituals**: When your inner child panics or aches, ask, *"What would I say to my daughter if she felt this way?"* Then say it to yourself.
- **Reclaiming Joy:**
  If you've ever struggled with this too, start simple. Each day, write down one thing that brings a smile, even if it's small: the sound of rain, a certain coffee mug, a cozy blanket, a favorite quote. You're not building a list to impress—you're remembering who you are.

🙏 Thriving Spiritually – Rooted, Not Rushed

Definition: To thrive spiritually means to be deeply rooted in God's presence, nourished by His Word, and responsive to His leading. It's living in alignment with His truth, not religion or performance, and walking in a relationship where growth flows from grace, not striving.

Spiritually: *"Blessed is the one... whose delight is in the law of the Lord, and who meditates on his law, day and night. That person is like a tree planted by streams of water..."* — Psalm 1:1–3

Spiritual thriving isn't flashy. It's not about being loud or perfect. It's about abiding. Staying. Remaining. Rooted in truth even when the storm rages. When your identity is grounded in God's Word, the world's lies lose their grip. When you walk with Him daily, you no longer chase moments of faith—you live them.

Clinically:
From a recovery and mental health standpoint, spiritual connection has been shown to reduce symptoms of anxiety, increase emotional resilience, and improve long-term healing outcomes for trauma survivors. According to research from the American Psychological Association, practices like prayer, worship, forgiveness, and spiritual reflection will positively affect the nervous system and brain function. Spiritually thriving is not about religious rituals—it's about relational rhythm.

My Story:
I used to think thriving spiritually meant getting it all right: reading the Bible every morning, praying perfectly, and saying the right things at the right time. I've learned instead that God isn't looking for perfection—He's looking for presence. He wants to have a relationship with me. Just like when I curled up in a ball on my couch and said, *"I'm climbing into your arms, Lord!"* and poured out the contents of my heart and mind to him.

There were seasons when I didn't even have the strength to pray in full sentences. All I had were tears and silence, but God heard me anyway. When all I could say was, *"Jesus."*
He met me in the stillness.

He met me in the mess.
And He never once walked away.

Now, thriving spiritually looks like starting my day with Scripture—
even if it's just one verse. It looks like pausing to worship God in the
car. Journaling prayers, crying on my knees, and trusting God with
the unseen seeds I'm planting. It looks like worship music in my car
and at home. It looks like taking the moment to thank Him every
chance I get.

I used to think God wanted a clean heart before I came to Him. Now
I know He wants all of it. The brokenness. The doubting. The
healing. The becoming.

Action Steps:

- **Start With One Verse**: Each day, write or speak one verse
  out loud. Let that be your anchor.
- **Contend in Prayer**: Set aside time for deep, focused prayer,
  where you talk and listen.
- **Create a Worship Ritual**: Begin or end your day with
  worship music, even if it's just one song. Let it shift the
  atmosphere.
- **Reflect, Don't Rush**: Journal what God is teaching you. Not
  what you "*should be doing,*" but what He's saying now.
- **Fast From the Noise**: Take breaks from comparison,
  performance, and distraction. Create space to hear His voice
  again.
- **Promises/Truths**: At the end of this book, I will share the list
  of promises I have written on an index card I carry. As soon
  as a lie creeps in, or as soon as the old worn-out tape starts
  to play, I can grab it and apply a truth.

Thriving spiritually isn't about storing enough faith to last a lifetime—it's about trusting God for today's portion. That truth came alive when I revisited the story of manna in the wilderness.

In Exodus 16, the Israelites wandered in the desert after being freed from slavery in Egypt. They were hungry, fearful, and unsure of what the future held. God, in His mercy, sent manna—a daily provision of bread from heaven, but there was a catch: they could only collect enough for that day. If they tried to store it for tomorrow, it would spoil.

God was teaching them something profound:

"I am your daily bread. I am your enough. Come back tomorrow, and I will still be faithful."

That lesson hit me deeply.

For so long, I tried to hoard strength. Predict outcomes. Plan my healing as if it were a checklist. But healing doesn't come in bulk—it comes in daily bread portions. It comes in today's grace. Today's peace. Today's whisper from the Holy Spirit reminds me that I am not alone.

Every time I pause for Scripture, every prayer I whisper, every moment of silence, every act of obedience—these are my manna moments. They're not flashy. They're not always emotionally charged. But they're faithful, consistent, life-giving. Over time, those moments seed the clouds of my life, creating the atmosphere where spiritual growth can rain down.

It's not about feeling it every time. It's about trusting that He's there every time.

So now, when I open my Bible in the morning, I remember: this is my daily bread.

When I pause to pray, I'm not just talking. I'm gathering manna.

When I worship, even when it's hard, I'm seeding the clouds.

When I say no to distractions and yes to truth, I'm creating space for spiritual rain to fall.

Healing doesn't just happen in the breakthrough moments. It's also in the manna moments—faithfully and consistently choosing God, every day.

📖 Reflection & Renewal: Journal and Action Steps

- **Exodus 16:4 (NIV):** *"I will rain down bread from heaven for you. The people are to go out each day and gather enough for that day."*

- **Psalm 1:3 (NIV):** *"That person is like a tree planted by streams of water, which yields its fruit in season…"*

- **Romans 12:2 (NIV):** *"Be transformed by the renewing of your mind."*

- **Zechariah 4:10 (NLT):** *"Do not despise these small beginnings, for the Lord rejoices to see the work begin."*

- **2 Corinthians 12:9 (NIV):** *"My grace is sufficient for you, for my power Is made perfect in weakness."*

Journal Prompts:

1. What does *"thriving"* mean to me today? How does it differ from how I've defined it in the past?

2. In what areas have I tried to hoard strength instead of trusting God for daily manna?

3. What lies have I believed about my worth, my body, or my healing? What truth do I want to speak instead?

4. Which of the four categories (Mentally, Physically, Emotionally, Spiritually) am I most grounded in right now? Which one is calling for more attention?

5. What are the small, daily practices that help me seed the clouds in my life? How can I commit to showing up for them?

✅ Next Steps to Walk Out Healing:

- **Create a Daily Seeding Routine:** List 1 action you'll take in each category—Mental, Physical, Emotional, and Spiritual—every day this week.

- **Write a "Manna Moment" Reflection Each Morning:** Ask, *"What do I need today?"* and *"Where is God providing*?" Then write it down.

- **Speak a Scripture Aloud Each Day:** Don't just read—declare. Let the Word become your daily cloud seed.

- **Start a "Not Mine" List:** Releasing what doesn't belong to you emotionally or spiritually creates space for thriving.

- **Check-In Weekly with Yourself:** Use a journal or trusted friend to reflect on progress and gently redirect where needed.

📑 Citations, Acknowledgments & Further Study:

- **Mark Batterson** – Win the Day: 7 Daily Habits to Help You Stress Less & Accomplish More, 2020, Multnomah (Penguin Random House LLC).
  – Inspiration for the cloud seeding metaphor and spiritual disciplines.

- **The Holy Bible** – Scripture excerpts from NIV and NLT versions, used to ground spiritual principles and daily application.

Clinical and Healing Resources:

- **Brené Brown** – *The Gifts of Imperfection and Atlas of the Heart – Concepts on Emotional Literacy, Shame, and Healing.*

- **Dr. Kristin Neff** – *Self-Compassion – Groundbreaking Research on How Kindness Transforms Healing.*

- **Bessel van der Kolk** – *The Body Keeps the Score – Understanding Trauma in the Body and Somatic Healing Practices.*

- **Dr. Marsha Linehan** – Creator of DBT (Dialectical Behavior Therapy), providing the foundation for emotional validation and regulation.

- **Albert Ellis & Aaron Beck** – Founders of REBT and CBT therapy models; tools for rewiring thought patterns and breaking mental strongholds.

Acknowledgments:

To every woman and man who has stared at a blank page, wondering what they love…

To those learning to reparent themselves, one truth at a time…
To the ones waking up each day trying again—**you are seeding the clouds, and the rain is coming.**

Thank you for trusting me with your story. You are not behind—you are becoming.

Chapter 8

Secrets Keep You Sick

"Sticks and stones may break my bones, but names (words) will never hurt me."

We all remember hearing that on the playground growing up. Chances are, we might have chanted it ourselves. If only that old childhood adage were true!

Sadly, sticks and stones may break my bones, but words can also wound me.

Words! They come to me in a flood. It's that little voice in the back of my head. It seems to pick the times I am already feeling under attack. It likes to bring up hurtful things people have said and flash images in my memory of times I would rather forget. It screams out every mistake and wrongdoing I have ever made. It reminds me of my past like a nagging record stuck on repeat. It is the voice of the kids not wanting to pick me for their teams. It is the voice of my ex-husband telling me that since I am so fat, my kids will be embarrassed by me and reject me. It is the voice of bullies picking on me for my clothes or my freckles. It is the countless other words that have been spoken over me or to me.

These things have become bricks in my suitcase. They are the ones I tend to default to. They tell me that nothing I do is good enough. That everything is my fault. That if I were smarter or prettier or kinder or if I just tolerated more or accepted things as they are and didn't expect more...... The list can go on and on. And I know I am not alone. I know that others can relate. It is the comments of *"you are as dumb as a box of rocks"*, *"are you stupid?"*, *"I am so embarrassed by you"* and countless other, sometimes even innocent comments, that added together became not so innocent in our minds. They have reduced us to a pile of rocks and sticks.

I have had more than a few times where these things have been overpowering. I have been faced with someone else's laundry list of things I did or didn't do. Regardless of their intent, it hurts. I found myself taking ownership of their junk. Then came my own words. Replaying what I should have, or could have done. I play it back like I can somehow change it, then play it forward, and imagine what could have happened. It is a horrible cycle. It perpetuates ideas that I should keep burying these things at the back of my closet. That, if people knew, what would they say? Before you know it, you are keeping everything to yourself. It feels like there's no safe place and no safe person.

Slowly, I started applying the truth. I made a list. I got quiet and made a list of all the things that play on the tape that is in my mind. Every secret. Every lie. I listed times and dates when I could. I listed who said or did these hurtful things. I listed how they made me feel. I had a big stack by the time it was done.

With tears streaming down my face, I walked to our fireplace and burned them! I watched them go up in flames. I am not bound by the things people say to me. I am not bound by my past. I am not bound by things others have done to me. Those things do not define me. I will not allow secrets to keep me sick, in bondage, fearful, or ashamed. I am not required to be stuck in a pattern that will allow someone else to belittle me. I do not have to accept what someone else wants me to believe about myself or my situation. I am not my sin. My mistakes do not define me. Someone else who needs to feel good about themselves or to blame me to find peace is not my problem. Someone else's denial does not constitute my acceptance of something that is not mine to own. I do not have to put up with disrespect or abuse, mentally, emotionally, or physically.

As the last of the papers disappeared...

I know that I must fill this space with truth. I know, because I have done this before. If I leave this space empty, the thoughts will creep back in. I must apply the truth daily. Just like food and water are essential for me to survive, the truth is that what I was created to crave will strengthen me and set me free and lead me to a purpose-driven life. The enemy wants nothing more than for me to believe that I do not matter. That it doesn't make a difference what little things I do right because I always fail. Good news! He is not the author or the finisher of my story! I looked up the promises, the truths God says about me. I began to write out each promise. I asked God to burn them into my heart. To replace every lie I had unpacked with a truth.

One of my favorite devotional writers, Mary Sutherland, said this in a devotion on our thought life:

"Thoughts are real and powerful! Our actions, our attitudes, our habits are born in the mind ... in our thought life. We can literally change our lives by changing what we think about. Isaiah 26:3 promises, 'You will keep in perfect peace all who trust in you, whose thoughts are fixed on you!' Peace and joy involve both the heart and the mind. Wrong thinking will lead to wrong living. The first step

toward a right thought life is to recognize the power of our thoughts."

She goes on to say, *"We must refuse lies and fill our minds with absolute truth – God's Word. As we digest it, as we take it into our lives and saturate our thoughts with it, we will be able to discern between truth and lies. Life-changing power is found in the Word of God!"*

I read once of a tourist who, while traveling to Alaska, during the building of the Alaskan pipeline, came across a road sign that read, *"Be careful which route you choose. You'll be in it for the next 200 miles."* We often allow negative thoughts to create a rut in our minds, giving them access to our lives. By filling our minds with scripture, we fill those old ruts with peace and create new *"ruts"* that soon become the right thought patterns. Then we begin thinking God's thoughts, and our thoughts become true.

One of the fiercest battles with depression is in my thought life. Yes, Satan is a liar! He wants to control my mind through his lies because, when I believe the truth, the Holy Spirit will take over. When I feed my thought life a steady diet of truth, I invite the Holy Spirit to work! When I believe a lie, Satan steps in! He sticks his hairy toe (I have never seen it, but I know it is ugly and hairy) into the walls of my mind, hurling his destruction into every step I take. Friend, the enemy will lie to you about the way you look, your relationships, your worth and identity, your fears and dreams, and your God. Do not surrender one inch of your thought life to him. Choose truth instead and stand firm!

"The mind is a garden that could be cultivated to produce the harvest that we desire.

The mind is a workshop where the important decisions of life and eternity are made.

154

The mind is an armory where we forge the weapons for our victory or our destruction.

The mind is a battlefield where all the decisive battles of life are won or lost."

— (Author unknown)

As you go through each day, identify and record any negative thoughts. Read each thought aloud. Determine why it is negative. Apply a promise from scripture to each thought and pray, asking God to re-train your mind.

Today, I was able to take every thought captive. Each one that came, I took captive and spoke the truth. When the lies crept in and the memories of things I kept secret reared their ugly heads, I spoke the truth. Sometimes it's just saying *"Nope, not today! I am taking everything thought captive."* My husband says I talk to myself a lot more these days. I laugh! I know it's really me speaking truth to the darkness.

Philippians 4:8 (NIVB) *"Finally, brothers, whatever is true, whatever is noble, whatever is right, whatever is pure, whatever is lovely, whatever is admirable–if anything is excellent or praiseworthy–think about such things."*

Maybe, today, you are struggling with all the reasons you don't measure up; if anyone knew the real you, you are sure they would shun you and push you away. Maybe you were told things that are just not true. Maybe things happened to you that haunt you and hurt you. Hurting people hurt people, and maybe, that is what has happened to you! Maybe, today, you need to take a piece of paper and write your statement of what you are worth and who you are! If by some chance you are reading this and you have nowhere to begin, I would love to pray for you, encourage you, and share the things God has shown me. Over the years, on more than one occasion, I wanted to end my life. It was the darkest place I have ever walked through, and had I not heard the voices of my children and the voice of my God, I am not sure I would be here today! I couldn't catch my breath. My eyes stung and my ears burned. I had hit bottom, and I never thought I would look up. Like the whisper of the wind, He came into my dark place and used many different things to show me I am not alone. I have value and I matter. I have said it before, and I will say it again, "*I am not my sins, my shortcomings, or my failures!*" And my friend, neither are you!

Let today be a new day- let God reaffirm to you exactly who you are! No more lies, no more fear.   A new day bathed in His amazing Grace!

Reflection & Renewal: Journal and Action Steps

Scriptures for Meditation:

- **John 8:32 (NIV):** *"Then you will know the truth, and the truth will set you free."*

- **Romans 5:8 (NIV):** *"But God demonstrates his own love for us in this: While we were still sinners, Christ died for us."*

- **2 Corinthians 10:5 (NIV):** *"...we take captive every thought to make it obedient to Christ."*

- **Philippians 4:8 (NIV):** *"Whatever is true... think about such things."*

- **Isaiah 43:18–19 (NIV):** *"Forget the former things; do not dwell on the past. See, I am doing a new thing!"*

✎ Journal Prompts:

1. What hurtful words or lies have longest echoed in my heart and mind? Write them down—uncensored.

2. What secrets have I kept out of shame, fear, or survival that need to be released to God?

3. What would it look like for me to forgive someone who never apologized? What would that release feel like?

4. What does God say about me that contradicts the lies I've believed? List 3 verses that speak directly to your identity.

5. What would I say if I could write a letter to the version of myself who carried those secrets the longest?

☑ Next Steps to Walk Out Healing:

- **Burn the Lies:** As described in the chapter, take a safe moment to write out the lies, labels, and secrets that have kept you sick. Then burn them—symbolically and prayerfully surrendering them to God. Say out loud, *"I am not these lies. I am who God says I am."*

- **Create a *"Truth Mirror"*:** Write Scriptures and affirmations about your identity in Christ on sticky notes and place them on your mirror, in your car, on your phone—wherever old thoughts try to sneak in.

- **Practice Forgiveness Daily:** Write a statement like, *"I forgive ___, not for them, but for my peace."* Repeat it when old wounds reopen. Forgiveness doesn't require reconciliation—it requires release.

- **Scripture Saturation:** Choose one promise from God each day. Read it, write it, speak it. Let it sink in and do the work of transformation.

- **Reach for Safe Community:** Healing loves company. Share this chapter, your story, or your prayer request with someone you trust—or bring it to God in journaling or prayer.

Citations, Acknowledgments & Further Study:

Devotional Excerpt:

- **Mary Southerland**, *Girlfriends in God Devotional* – on renewing the mind and cultivating truth-based thought patterns. Quoted with attribution under fair use for educational reflection.

Scriptural Foundation:

- Scriptures referenced from the New International Version (NIV) of the Holy Bible.

Recommended Reading:

- *Battlefield of the Mind* – Joyce Meyer
- *Switch On Your Brain* – Dr. Caroline Leaf
- *Forgiving What You Can't Forget* – Lysa TerKeurst
- *Breaking Free* – Beth Moore
- *Emotionally Healthy Spirituality* – Peter Scazzero

Acknowledgment:

To every woman and man who has sat in silence, hiding the weight of words never meant to define her, this chapter was written for you. You are not your secrets. You are not your shame. You are God's beloved. This is your new beginning.

Chapter 9

Healing from My Past

I've spent most of my life holding myself to a standard I would never place on another person. The grace I preached, the compassion I gave, the forgiveness I extended—it somehow didn't apply to me.

Everyone else could make mistakes and still be loved. Everyone else could fall and get back up. But me? I held onto guilt like it was my penance. I replayed every misstep, every moment, "I *should have known better*," like I could somehow undo them if I punished myself long enough. That's the lie I lived under: that healing was for others, but consequences were mine to carry alone.

Forgiveness from God? I believed in it. Forgiveness from others? I hoped for it. But forgiving myself? That felt impossible.

For a long time, I didn't realize that not forgiving myself was just another form of control. If I stayed angry at myself, I thought I could somehow protect myself from repeating the pain. But shame is not a safety net. It's a prison. And I was the one keeping myself locked inside.

I had to come face to face with the truth: I cannot heal from a past I keep punishing myself for. Healing meant laying it down. Not just the parts others saw. Not just the clean, church-friendly version. All of it.

The abuse I stayed silent about.
The times I lost my temper.
The seasons I wasn't the mother I wanted to be.

The years I tried to earn love by being who they wanted me to be, not who God made me to be.

The choices I made out of desperation, fear, or loneliness.

The nights I cried myself to sleep, wishing I could go back in time and do things differently.

But I can't go back.

And I don't need to.

Because Jesus didn't come for my perfection. He came for my redemption.

Before we go any further, I want to stop and take a deep breath with you.

If you've made it to this point in the book, you've also made it through some of the hardest parts of my story—and maybe your own. You've stood with me as I unpacked suitcases of shame, exposed secrets, tore down false scripts, faced addiction, survived betrayal, and learned how to thrive in places where I once just barely survived.

We've discussed trauma, truth, recovery, identity, grace, and growth. We've wept, questioned, prayed, and hoped. Now, at last, we arrive at one of the most sacred parts of the journey: learning to forgive myself and truly heal from my past.

Not just face it. Not just talk about it. Heal. Because carrying the pain isn't the same as healing from it. Naming the wounds is only part of the story. Healing means inviting God into the places we'd rather keep locked away. It means extending grace, not just outward, but inward. That meant facing the hardest person to forgive: me.

Because Jesus didn't come for my perfection, He came for my redemption.

And part of that redemption is learning to see my motherhood through His eyes.

I have four children from my first marriage, my husband has two from his, and together we have one. So, yes—we have seven total. A beautiful, blended, imperfect family, stitched together by grace, growth, and more prayer than I could ever measure. Blending families is never easy. Add in trauma, addiction, loss, and survival, and it becomes something even more complex. Sacred. Messy. Holy.

I've struggled deeply with shame over what my kids had to walk through. The things they saw. The seasons they endured. The chaos they didn't choose, but had to live through anyway. I've lain awake at night replaying every word I wish I could take back, every time I lost my temper, and every moment I shut down from the weight of it all.

Parenting doesn't come with a manual. There's no how-to guide for blending broken pieces into something whole, but I did my best. Still—it felt like it wasn't enough.

What hurt the most were the outside voices. Ones who looked at my children's lives and decided it all must have been a tragedy. Ones that said things like, *"Your poor kids. I feel so bad they had to go through all of that."* Those comments were daggers. Not just because they hurt, but because they confirmed what I already believed: that I had failed.

I already thought I was a bad mom. That they were going to be ashamed of me—my body, my choices, my past—and when others spoke it aloud, it wasn't just painful—it was paralyzing. I didn't need a chorus of critics—I had a courtroom inside my mind replaying the charges daily. Every word spoken *"at me"* wasn't just commentary. A confirmation of the lie I had already internalized: I had ruined everything.

So, I shut down. I pulled back. I tried to overcompensate—to fix it all, and make up for every mistake. But that didn't bring healing. It only deepened the exhaustion. That's when I began to understand something that changed how I saw those reactions, not just from others, but from myself.

I learned that what I was experiencing was a form of psychological conditioning—emotional Pavlovian response. Pavlov's famous experiments proved that dogs could be trained to associate a neutral stimulus (a bell) with a significant event (food). Over time, the dogs would salivate at the sound of the bell alone.

In trauma survivors like me—and maybe like you—criticism, shame, and disapproval become the *"bell."* Even small triggers—a sideways comment, a disappointed look, or a memory—provoke intense emotional responses—not because the situation itself is always catastrophic, but because the emotional memory behind it has trained your nervous system to expect rejection, danger, or failure.

It's what psychologists call emotional conditioning, and when combined with repeated invalidation or abuse, it reinforces a core belief that you are unworthy, unsafe, and always at fault.

So, when people spoke gracelessly about my parenting, or my family's past, it wasn't just hurtful. It was physiologically re-traumatizing. I was *"salivating at the bell"*—bracing for pain, rejection, or condemnation, even when it wasn't justified. I had become conditioned to expect pain and to accept blame—even when it wasn't mine to carry.

But here's what I'm learning: healing rewrites the response. And grace breaks the cycle.

I no longer have to live at the mercy of others' perceptions or comments. I no longer have to prove my worth through perfection or silence. I can acknowledge what was hard, what was broken, and what was true, without being defined by it.

At times, when my guilt was suffocating—when it gripped my chest so tightly, I couldn't breathe—I would reach out to my kids.

Sometimes it was to say, *"I love you. I'm proud of you."* Other times, it was me breaking under the weight of it all, and reaching out to say, *"I'm sorry."* Sorry for not being a better mom. Sorry for the seasons I didn't speak up, while trying to keep the peace. Sorry for the times I withdrew, retreated, and went silent—not because I didn't care, but because I didn't know how to deal with the pain.

I would sob. I would try to hold myself together long enough to finish the sentence. Every single time, they would say the same thing:

"Mom, we love you. We know you did the best you could."

But I couldn't accept that—at least, not right away. How could they mean that? How could they say that when I knew the junk I had packed into their lives? The things they had to carry because of what we walked through. I had one shot, I thought. One chance to protect them, to give them the childhood I never had—and I blew it.

But here's what I've come to understand, through therapy, through prayer, and many teary late-night conversations with God:

No parent is perfect.

We are all doing our best with the pieces we've been handed—often broken, jagged, or incomplete. We're trying to build something steady in a world that keeps shaking. We're navigating uncharted territory, under the constant barrage of new challenges, unexpected pain, and unresolved pasts.

We are not perfect, but we are present, and sometimes that's where the miracle starts.

My two oldest boys have tender and deep hearts. They've sat with me in some of those sacred, aching conversations—where the tears flow without shame, and the truth rises, unfiltered. They've told me how proud they are of me. They admire the woman I've become and recognize my fight to heal, grow, and love well, acknowledging how these hardships have shaped them into the men and fathers they are today.

They have said, *"Mom, it wasn't all bad. You were there. You showed up. And we love you."*

And I've finally begun to believe them.

Healing doesn't erase the past—it reframes it. It lets us see not just what was broken but what was built. It reminds us that love can grow in the cracks. Even in the mess, God was planting seeds of strength, compassion, and resilience into my children's hearts.

They didn't just survive. They became who they are because of the road we walked, not despite it.

And I'm learning to forgive myself... because they already have.

Their forgiveness has opened the door to something deeper—real conversation. Not surface-level pleasantries or mother-son catch-ups, but honest, sacred space where we talk about the hard things—what we've all carried, how we've been hurt, healed, and hoped, and what we want our legacy to be.

You see, healing isn't just to give me back my voice. It is to give them theirs, too.

We've talked about faith and what it means to walk with God even when the road is dark and full of detours, to break generational patterns, not through perfection, but through presence and prayer. We've talked about how they want to raise their children differently—and yet, how grateful they are for how I kept showing up, even when it felt like I was failing.

They've told me that the strength they now have—the empathy, the awareness, the heart for their families—came from watching me fight for healing. They've seen me cry out to God. They've seen me repent, repair, and rebuild. And those aren't weaknesses to them. They're witnesses of what grace looks like in action. That's the legacy I'm passing on now.

Not a legacy of perfection, or one where I pretended that we had it all together, but a legacy of faithfulness—of continuing to rise, choose healing, inviting God into every broken space, and asking Him to make it whole.

Because that's what He does.

"He heals the brokenhearted and binds up their wounds." —Psalm 147:3

"The righteous man walks in his integrity; his children are blessed after him." —Proverbs 20:7

My kids are living proof that God can bring beauty from ashes—not because I got it all right, but because I finally stopped trying to do it alone.

If you're reading this and you've carried guilt over the way you've raised your children, the things they've seen or heard, or the struggles they've endured—I see you, and I want you to listen to what I'm saying:

"You are not too late. You are not too broken. And it is not too far gone."

Your willingness to heal, apologize, show up, and invite truth and grace into your home is already rewriting your family story.

Healing is the legacy. Grace is the inheritance. Restoration is the gift we give—not because we earned it, but because we were bold enough to receive it.

There are still wounds my children carry.

There are still memories that sting—some they've spoken out loud, some they've tucked away, and some I can see written across their faces in moments when the past unexpectedly resurfaces. I feel it. I know they do, too. And while I wish I could go back and rewrite those scenes—protect them from what they saw, soften what they felt, hold them tighter in the chaos—I can't.

What I can do is acknowledge it. Speak it out loud. Own it without excuses and love them without conditions.

I did my best, but that may not be enough for everyone. Some people might look at our story and see only the mess. They might judge the middle without knowing the miracle, and that's okay. That's not mine to carry.

What is mine to carry is this truth: healing is personal. I cannot force it, demand I, or complete it for someone else, including my children.

There comes a point in every healing journey that the responsibility to unpack what was handed to us becomes ours. While that might sound harsh, it's actually freeing. It means we get to choose what we do with what we were given. We may not have chosen the pain, but we can decide what comes next.

So, as I continue healing, I pray for them to find their path of healing, their relationship with truth, and their understanding of grace. I pray that they look back, not with bitterness, but with bravery. That they remember not just the hard, but the hope. Not just the pain, but the perseverance. They see a mom who got it wrong many times... but never gave up. Not on them. Not on God. Not on herself.

This isn't about pretending our past didn't happen. It's about believing that our past doesn't get the final say.

Before we close this chapter, I want to pause and acknowledge something: I couldn't have done any of this without the relentless and redemptive love of God.

Through every chapter of my story—through every wound, every secret, every tear-soaked moment—God was there. When I felt unworthy of love, He reminded me I was chosen. When I was drowning in shame, He whispered grace. When I thought I had to carry the consequences of my past alone, He lifted the weight I could no longer bear. I didn't find healing through willpower or self-help books. I found it in the presence of a Savior who never gave up on me.

God wasn't just part of my healing. He was healing.
Every step forward I've taken has been because of Him. Every lie I've laid down has been replaced with His truth. Every ounce of freedom I now walk in? It's because Jesus paid the price, invited me in, and held my heart through every breaking and every rebuilding.

If you're reading these words and feel like you're too far gone, too broken, or too much—you are not. I promise you, there is no chapter so dark that God can't redeem it. There is no pain so deep that He can't reach it. No story is so messy that He can't turn it into a message of grace and hope.

If you're ready to take the next step, I'd love to pray with you.

🙏 Prayer to Invite Christ in: Turning My Mess into a Message of Grace and Hope

Father God,
I come to You just as I am—no mask, no performance, and no pretending. I've tried to carry this life, this pain, this past by my own strength for far too long. I'm tired, Lord. I've reached the end of myself, and I realize now that was the starting place you were waiting for.

Today, I open the door of my heart and invite you in—not just to visit, but to stay. Jesus, I believe You died for my sins and rose again to offer me new life. I want to receive that gift. I want to receive You. Wash me clean, heal my heart, and rewrite my story with the truth of who You say I am.

Take every piece of my past—the shattered, the scarred, the secret—and use it for good. Let my mess become a message of mercy. Let the pain I've walked with become a pathway of hope for someone else. Lord, I want to live a life that reflects Your grace, power, and unrelenting love.

Today I surrender. Today I chose You.
In Jesus' Name, Amen.

Forgiving ourselves is often the hardest step. It's one thing to believe that God can forgive us, and even that others might, but to offer that same grace inward, to our hearts? That feels impossible after we've been carrying shame for so long. We replay what we wish we'd done differently and hold ourselves hostage to a past we can't change. Here's the truth—God never called us to be perfect— He called us to be redeemed. If He, in all His holiness, chooses to extend mercy to us, who are we to deny it? Self-forgiveness isn't about excusing what's been done—it's about surrendering it to the One who already paid for it. It's about accepting the grace, freely offered, and finally letting go. This next prayer is one I prayed with trembling hands and tear-filled eyes. I invite you to pray with me now.

🙏 Prayer of Self-Forgiveness: Releasing the Guilt, Receiving the Grace

Dear Jesus,
You know me better than anyone. You've seen it all—every choice, every misstep, every moment I wish I could take back, and yet, You never turned away. Your love never left. Your grace was never out of reach.

Still, I've struggled to forgive myself. I've clung to guilt as if it were justice. I've replayed mistakes like they were permanent markers on my worth. But today, Lord, I choose to let go.

I forgive myself—not because I deserve it, but because you already paid the price. I release the weight of shame I've been carrying. I lay down the burden of my past and receive the truth: I am forgiven. I am redeemed. I am free.

Help me walk in that freedom, even when it's hard. When the enemy whispers old lies, remind me of Your Word. When guilt creeps back in, remind me of the cross. I won't rewrite what You've already redeemed. I won't punish myself for what You've already pardoned.

Thank You for loving me so fully. Help me to love myself with that same grace.

In Your name I pray,
Amen.

Reflection & Renewal: Journal and Action Steps

- *Therefore, there is now no condemnation for those who are in Christ Jesus."* — Romans 8:1

- *"As far as the east is from the west, so far has he removed our transgressions from us."* — Psalm 103:12

- *"Though your sins are like scarlet, they shall be as white as snow."* — Isaiah 1:18

- *"Create in me a clean heart, O God, and renew a right spirit within me."* — Psalm 51:10

- *"Even if we feel guilty, God is greater than our feelings, and he knows everything."* — 1 John 3:20 (NLT)

Journal Prompts:

1. Where have you been the hardest on yourself, and why?

2. What does self-forgiveness look like in your life today?

3. What are the specific memories, regrets, or choices you are holding onto?

4. How might extending grace to yourself reflect God's heart more fully?

5. Who or what has helped you believe that healing is possible?

6. Write a letter to your younger self. What truth does he/she need to hear today?

✅ Next Steps to Walk Out Healing:

- Choose one area of your past that still weighs on you. Write it down. Pray over it. Then release it—burn it, tear it up, or bury it as a symbolic surrender to God.

- Write out 3 truths from Scripture that contradict the lies you've believed about yourself. Keep them visible this week.

- Begin using the phrase, *"That was then. This is now,"* when past guilt tries to creep in. Speak life over yourself out loud.

- Schedule a grace date—a time where you do something kind, restorative, and healing for you. Not as a reward, but as a practice of grace.

- Consider talking with your children or loved ones honestly, without over-apologizing. Speak truth, express love, and listen with humility.

📖 Citations & Further Study:

- Neff, Kristin. *Self-Compassion: The Proven Power of Being Kind to Yourself*. William Morrow, 2011.

- Cloud, Henry & Townsend, John. *Boundaries: When to Say Yes, How to Say No to Take Control of Your Life*. Zondervan, 1992.

- Brene Brown. *The Gifts of Imperfection.* Hazelden Publishing, 2010.

- Celebrate Recovery®. Participant Guides 1–4. Life's Healing Choices Curriculum.

- Bible Gateway. Various scriptures sourced from NIV, NLT, and ESV translations.

Chapter 10:

Embracing Your New Identity

Before we step fully into the light of this final chapter, I want to take a moment to pause and look back—not to dwell, but to remember how far we've come.

This book began with a suitcase. Heavy with shame, silence, trauma, and grief, I dragged it through every chapter of my life— through pain I didn't deserve and mistakes I wish I could take back. From unpacking wounds in Chapter 1 to walking through recovery, forgiveness, and identity, this story has been about becoming—not the becoming where it's tied to perfection or performance, but instead, the slow, sacred kind that happens when truth replaces lies and grace takes root.

Each chapter has stripped something away—a false belief, an old narrative, a secret that once held power. In their place, new foundations have been laid. Grace. Healing. Truth. Boundaries. Redemption. Stepping into this final chapter, I want to shout from the rooftops: I am not who I used to be.

In 2023, I began what I called my reset. I didn't know then how deeply it would affect every layer of my being. Emotionally, mentally, spiritually, and physically, I began again—not with a blank slate, but with the courage to rewrite the script. Since that moment, I've lost 126 pounds of physical weight, and what feels like 10,000 pounds of mental and emotional baggage.

I now take every thought captive. Every moment. Every day. When the lies creep in, I hurl truth right back at the enemy of my soul. I set boundaries. I use my voice. I protect my peace. I've learned that healing isn't passive—it's active. And freedom? It's a fight worth showing up for.

Recently, I bought the cutest little carry-on suitcase for a trip. That may not seem like a big deal, but as I packed—three outfits without hesitation—I felt a surge of victory. For so long, I feared clothes. Feared mirrors. Feared being seen. Buying them? That's still a work in progress. But I see her now—the woman I'm becoming. I'm learning to embrace her, not edit her.

I've attacked food fear head-on with the help of Travis Wallace and Sofia Perez through The FR4MULA, a journey that's been about so much more than macros or meal plans. It's about freedom. Travis always says, reinvention is a requirement—and I've taken that to heart. I meet weekly with my amazing therapist, who has walked beside me as I peel back the layers, and God... Well, He's woven every thread together.

He's brought the right people into my path at the right time. He spoke the truth to me when I couldn't hear it. He has reminded me again and again: I belong to Him.

This chapter is the victory lap. It's the anthem. It's the declaration that grace wins, healing is possible, and the old me is gone. I am living proof of what happens when we stop surviving and start becoming.

If you know me, you know that sports—especially baseball—have always played a big part in our family. My youngest son played through college until an injury in 2019 forced him off the field. I can still picture him stepping up to the plate, laser-focused, head high. A lot of players have a walk-up song echoing through the stadium as they approach the plate. Announcing their moment. Their anthem. Their declaration that they are ready to face whatever pitch comes their way.

And now? It's my walk-up moment.

If I had a walk-up song for life, it would be Megan Woods' "*The Truth.*" Every lyric connects like when a ball meets the sweet spot on the bat—pure, powerful, and full of purpose. Every time I hear that song on the radio, I sing it loud and in person. I changed the "*He*" to "*You,*" because I'm singing it directly to the God who never gave up on me. This song isn't just music—it's a battle cry. It's the anthem of the new me, who knows who she is and stares down the lies and chosen truth.

"The Truth"
Written by Jeff Pardo, Matthew West, Megan Woods
© Capitol CMG Publishing

> *How many times can you hear the same lie*
> *Before you start to believe it?*
> *The enemy keeps whisperin' to me*
> *I swear these days, it's all that I'm hearin'*
>
> *I used to know who I was*
> *Now I look in the mirror and I'm not so sure*
> *Lord, I don't wanna listen to the lies anymore*

(Chorus)

The truth is, I am my Father's child
I make Him proud, and I make Him smile
I was made in the image of a perfect King
He looks at me and wouldn't change a thing
The truth is, I am truly loved
By a God who's good when I'm not good enough
I don't belong to the lies, I belong to You
And that's the truth

When I feel like there's so much noise
Livin' rent-free in my head
Heaven finds me in a still, small voice
And it sounds like grace instead

You remind me who I am
When I look in the mirror, and I'm not so sure
Lord, I don't wanna listen to the lies anymore

(Chorus)

The truth is, I am my Father's child
I make Him proud, and I make Him smile
I was made in the image of a perfect King
He looks at me and wouldn't change a thing
The truth is, I am truly loved
By a God who's good when I'm not good enough
I don't belong to the lies, I belong to You
And that's the truth

(Bridge)

I know who I am 'cause I know who You are
And I hold Your truth inside of my heart
I know the lies are always gonna try and find me
But I've never been so sure

182

(Chorus)
The truth is, I am my Father's child
I make Him proud, and I make Him smile
I was made in the image of a perfect King
He looks at me and wouldn't change a thing
The truth is, I am truly loved
By a God who's good when I'm not good enough
I don't belong to the lies, I belong to You
And that's the truth

(Outro)
And that's the truth

Now it's your turn.

Maybe you've been carrying the weight of your past, listening to lies, shrinking yourself to fit into places God never asked you to stay. But what if today is your walk-up moment? What if this is where you dig your feet in, lift your head high, and step into the batter's box of your own becoming? Friend, the truth is—you are not what you've been through. You are who God says you are. So, turn up the anthem. Sing it loud, and step into the fullness of your identity. It's time to walk out in truth.

📖 Reflection & Renewal: Journal and Action Steps

📄 Scriptures for Meditation:

- 2 Corinthians 5:17 – *"Therefore, if anyone is in Christ, he is a new creation. The old has passed away; behold, the new has come."*

- Romans 8:1 – *"There is therefore now no condemnation for those who are in Christ Jesus."*

- Galatians 2:20 – *"I have been crucified with Christ. It is no longer I who lives, but Christ who lives in me."*

- Ephesians 2:10 – *"For we are God's masterpiece. He has created us anew in Christ Jesus, so we can do the good things he planned for us long ago."*

- Psalm 139:14 – *"I praise You because I am fearfully and wonderfully made; Your works are wonderful; I know that full well."*

Journal Prompts:

1. What are the lies you've believed about your identity? Where did they start?

2. How do you see yourself differently now than you did when you began this book?

3. What truths do you need spoken over yourself daily to stay rooted in God's promises?

4. What would a *"walk-up song"* for your life sound like right now?

5. Who do you need to become for the next chapter of your journey? What does it look like to walk boldly into that identity?

☑ Next Steps to Walk Out Healing:

- Choose one Scripture from the list above to meditate on each morning this week.

- Write an "*I Am*" statement—your declaration of truth rooted in God's Word.

- Share one piece of your healing journey with a trusted friend, mentor, or group.

- Create a playlist of songs that speak life and truth into your soul—songs you'll play when the lies try to sneak in.

- Write a letter to your future self, reminding her of who she is and what she's overcome.

📑 Citations, Acknowledgments & Further Study:

- *"The Truth"* by Megan Woods, Jeff Pardo, Matthew West | Lyrics licensed via LyricFind © Capitol CMG Publishing.

- The FR4MULA – Travis Wallace & Sofia Perez | for nutritional guidance, faith-driven transformation, and food freedom coaching.

- Celebrate Recovery | www.celebraterecovery.com

- Boundaries by Dr. Henry Cloud and Dr. John Townsend

- Renewing the Mind – Romans 12:2, foundational for the practice of replacing lies with truth

- Clinical and spiritual integration through ongoing therapy with Dr. Reese—thank you for being a safe place, a guiding voice, and a true partner in this journey of healing.

Conclusion

There came a moment when I knew—I couldn't keep going like this. Emotionally, mentally, spiritually, and physically, I was drowning. I was exhausted from dragging chains behind me that were never mine to carry in the first place. My mind was filled with lies, my heart heavy with guilt, and my body bearing the toll of it all. Then one day, I made a decision.

I chose freedom.

I chose to lay it all down—every lie, every secret, and every mask— then walk boldly toward healing. With the guidance of my therapist, I began to live with intention. I started asking myself hard questions and refusing to settle for halfway healing. I realized I mattered. I didn't need to look to others to define me or fix me. I was good enough—not in the world's eyes, but in God's.

I am the one He left the ninety-nine for. And if you're still reading, you are too.

At the start of 2023, I chose to reset. I began rebuilding my life brick by brick—mentally, emotionally, spiritually, and physically. As of today, I've lost 126 pounds of weight—but more than that, I've shed 10,000 pounds of mental and emotional baggage. I'm not who I used to be. I take every thought captive. I speak the truth out loud. I use my voice and protect my peace. I set boundaries and I write new scripts. I packed a tiny suitcase for a recent trip and felt a wave of victory when I folded three outfits into it—no shame, no hesitation.

I'm attacking food fear head-on with the help of Travis Wallace and Sofia Perez at The FR4MULA. God, in His goodness, brought them into my life right on time. Travis's words echo within my soul: *"Reinvention is a requirement."* I'm living proof that reinvention is not only possible—it's powerful.

Each day now, I choose grace. I choose intention. I choose truth.

I wrote the following declaration and taped it to my fridge. I read it daily—sometimes multiple times. It's not just words—it's my anchor.

My Daily Declaration

I have to choose forgiveness and grace consciously.

I have to make a decision to lay down the past and pick up my healing.

I have to make a choice to realize that I have a voice, an opinion, and they matter.

I have to make a choice to know that people can hurt me, but they have no right to and should not be allowed to.

I have to choose to make decisions that honor God and protect my family.

I have to affirm that I am worth it. That I matter. That I am good enough.

I have to realize: everyone doesn't have to like me, and I don't have to meet every expectation.

I have rights.

I have a voice.

I am not my past.

I am not defined by secrets or sin.

I am important.

My ideas, feelings, dreams, and goals matter.

I am forgiven.

I am completely known and fully loved by God.

I am a daughter of the King of Kings.

Made in His image.

I make Him smile.

And when He looks at me, He wouldn't change a thing.

Not at 54. Not ever.

So now I ask you...

What is it that grips your soul and holds you back?

What fear, lie, regret, or burden do you keep rehearsing in your mind?

What is your one thing that rises up and whispers, *"You'll never be free from this"*?

Write it down. Take out a piece of paper. At the top, name it. And then draw a line down the middle.

On one side: **LIES**
On the opposite side: **TRUTH**

Be honest. Let the lies spill out. Counter them with Scripture, with affirmations, with the voice of heaven that has never once spoken condemnation over you.

If you need help, visit the link to Bible Gateway on my website. Search for God's truth about your thing. Find the verses that speak life. Post them. Memorize them. Let them drown out the noise. Let them seed the clouds of your becoming.

Write your walk-out song. Your anthem. Your affirmation.

Don't go it alone.

Share with a friend. Speak it aloud. Reach out to someone you trust. Speak about what has kept you bound, because when secrets lose their silence, they lose their power, and healing takes root.

If you don't know where to begin? Begin here.

Pray. Open your mouth and speak honestly to the God who already knows and still says, *"Come."*

"Pick up your mat and walk…"
– John 5:8

Steve Arterburn says it beautifully in Healing Is a Choice:
"Pick up your mat and cry. Or pray. Or go to a meeting. Or take your medication. Or help someone else. Just pick up your life and experience all that God has for you."

Today is the day.

Not perfect. Not easy. But it is worth it.

Because you are worth it.

And me? I'm off to bake an angel food cake. The cream cheese frosting is softening on the counter. I'll dollop it generously—four or five heaping spoons—and savor each bite—a sweet, messy, and joyful reminder of the lavish grace that saved my life.

This is your time.
This is your walk-up moment.
This is your new beginning.

Let's go.

"Life is short. Break the rules. Forgive quickly. Kiss slowly. Love Truly. Laugh uncontrollably. Never regret anything that makes you smile."
-Mark Twain

📖 Final Acknowledgements Today

To every reader who picked up this book, opened their heart, and walked through the pages with me   thank you. I don't take it lightly. This was not just my story, it was an invitation into yours. Whether you saw reflections of yourself in these chapters or found encouragement for someone you love, my deepest prayer is that you walked away with one undeniable truth: you are not alone, and healing is possible.

I'm forever grateful to my family—my children, my grandchildren, my husband, and our blended, beautiful chaos—for loving me even when I couldn't always love myself. To my therapist, Dr. Reece— your wisdom, presence, and grace were a lifeline when I needed it most. To Travis Wallace and Sofia Perez of The FR4MULA—thank you for helping me face my fears around food and reclaim my health. You are part of my miracle.

To my community, to every friend who stood in the gap and prayed me through, and to the women and men who opened up their wounds and stood shoulder-to-shoulder with me in healing, thank you for holding space.

Above all, to my Savior—Jesus—who left the ninety-nine to find me... I give You all the glory. Every page of this book is a testimony to Your relentless love.

Now, friend, as you move forward, let this be more than just a good read. Let it be your turning point. Let it be the moment you say, *"This ends with me. This begins with Him."* Unpack that suitcase.

✅ Action Steps for You Today — Remember GRACE:

G – Give yourself permission to heal from the past.
You are not defined by your wounds, past sins, or mistakes. You are not your lowest moment. You are who God says you are.

R – Release the lies you've believed about yourself and replace them with truths.
Take every thought captive. Speak life. Write it. Post it. Pray it.

A – Allow grace to cover your mistakes, secrets, and struggles.
Forgiveness sets you free—whether it's forgiving yourself or others.

C – Choose to rewrite the script you tell yourself.
Stop living under the old narrative. Start speaking the one rooted in purpose, power, and possibility. Seed the clouds daily—and watch the blessings rain down.

E – Embrace the journey of healing with courage.
You don't have to be perfect to begin. Grace is your daily portion. It was paid for on the cross—and it's free.

To My Children,

If you're reading this, I want you to know something I've probably said a hundred times—and maybe should've said a hundred more:

I love you. I'm proud of you. And I'm sorry.

There are things I wish I could go back and do differently. There are moments I look back on and grieve—because you deserved more. You deserved a mom who wasn't carrying so much of her own pain, a mom who had learned how to speak up, show up, and stand strong sooner.

But here's what I need you to know:

I never stopped trying. Even when I was falling apart, I was fighting for you. I know I made mistakes, and I'm not asking you to pretend they didn't happen. I'm asking that you see the truth beneath the mess and that everything I did was from love. I was broken, not indifferent. I was hurting, not absent in heart. I was trying to survive a storm while carrying the umbrella over your heads.

I've asked your forgiveness before, and you gave it more generously than I ever gave it to myself. Your words, grace, and love reached places inside me I thought were too far gone.

I carry your hugs, your late-night talks, and your *"I'm proud of you, Mom,"* statements like treasures buried in my soul. You've told me I helped shape you into the men and women you are today—and hearing that? It's holy. It's healing. It's the whisper of redemption in the places where I once only heard regret.

I didn't do it perfectly, but I did it with everything I had. I'm still here. I'm still learning. I'm still showing up. I'm still growing.

And I'll always be in your corner—cheering you on, praying over you, and believing in the future God has for you.

Because I don't just love you…

I see you. I cherish you. And I'm so grateful to be your mom.

Mom

To My Children's Spouses and My Grandchildren,

You may never fully know what it means to me that you are a part of our family story.

To my daughters- and sons-in-law—you chose my children. You love them, build with them, cry with them, and walk beside them through the very life chapters I once prayed they'd have the strength to write. You hold space for their memories, for their dreams, and even for their scars. In loving them, you have also loved me—sometimes knowingly, sometimes unknowingly.

I know it hasn't always been easy. I know there may have been moments where the past crept in, where old pain showed up in new ways. But you stayed. You believed in them. You are building a life with them. And for that, I want to say thank you. From the depths of a mother's heart, thank you for seeing who they are, not just who they've been.

You are now part of our healing story. And your place in it is sacred.

And to my beautiful grandchildren—my precious, joy-filled, purpose-packed legacy:

Grammie loves you more than words could ever fully say.

You are the laughter in our family now. The wild imaginations, the tender hearts, the reminders of how good God is. You are the prayers I once whispered in the middle of the night, and now running barefoot through the answered light of day.

I need you to know something—something I pray you'll never forget:

You are not what the world says about you.
You are not what others may try to label or limit you with.

You are fearfully and wonderfully made.
You carry the light of generations of faith, perseverance, and grace.
You will change the world, not because life will always be easy, but because you were born with purpose, and on purpose.

When you read these pages one day and see the places Grammie got it wrong, I hope you also see the God who kept showing up to make things right. I hope you know that the same God who healed your Grammie wants to walk every step with you, too.

I love you deeply. I pray for you daily. I believe in your future.
I'll be the loudest one clapping—whether it's your first steps, your graduation march, or your quiet courage on a hard day.

You are my heart. You are my why.
And my love for you will always be home.

Leslie

To My Husband,

I could begin this letter in thousands of ways, but the most honest way to start is here: Thank you!

Thank you for staying.
Thank you for fighting—for us, for yourself, for our family, and for the healing we both so desperately needed.
Thank you for saying yes to grace, again and again, even when it was hard, messy, and painful.

There were days we didn't know if we'd make it. Days that I wasn't sure how we'd survive another conversation, another hurt, another night of silence or chaos or confusion. And yet, here we are—not because we were perfect, but because God was present.

We've seen the worst in each other. We've wept, yelled, withdrawn, and collapsed—and through it all, we've risen. We've clawed our way back—to love, truth, freedom, and faith. You stood beside me in my unraveling and held me in moments where words couldn't reach. I have watched you—broken and beautiful—rise from the ashes of addiction, reclaim your life, and become a man of integrity, strength, and honor.

You have been my reminder that redemption is real. Those second chances are sacred. That marriage is not a fairytale—it's a battlefield where the covenant wins. Every day you walked in recovery, every time you owned your mistakes, every prayer, every meeting, every moment you put your family first—you've preached the gospel louder than a thousand sermons.

I know we both carry regrets. I know there are things we wish we could go back and undo or redo. But I also know this: We are not who we were. I wouldn't trade what we've learned or the grace we've found for a cleaner story. Because this story—our story—has power. And I'm proud of it. I'm proud of us.

You are not the man I met. You are the man God called you to become, and I love him with every fiber of my being.

Thank you for loving me in my undoing.
Thank you for choosing me despite my flaws and failures.
Thank you for being the father, the partner, the fighter I prayed for—even when I didn't know how to ask for it.

You are my answered prayer. You are my safe place. And I still choose you.

Today. Tomorrow. Always.

Love,

Your wife

(Still yours—even when life was messy. Especially then.)

Dear Mom, Dad, and My Family,

As I've journeyed through the pages of this book—and through some of the deepest parts of my heart—I felt led to pause and write this letter to you. It's a letter not just of reflection, but of gratitude, honor, and love.

One of the earliest and most powerful memories etched into my soul is the moment you both gave your lives to Christ when I was just five years old. That moment marked the beginning of a legacy. It planted seeds of faith that would grow quietly and powerfully through every season of my life.

I was raised in a praying home, a home where the name of Jesus was spoken not just in church but in our daily life. I watched you seek Him—not perfectly, but purposefully. That foundation mattered more than I ever realized at the time. It shaped me. It steadied me. And it is part of the reason I am able to walk in healing and hope today.

To my extended family—thank you for being a support system of love and prayer. For every time you've shown up, whispered a prayer, spoken encouragement, or simply loved me through the valleys—you've been a part of this story too.

This letter is not about unpacking the past. It's about honoring the deep roots I've come from. It's about acknowledging the quiet prayers I didn't even know were being prayed over me. It's about recognizing that faith was modeled long before I could name it— and it became the anchor in the storms of life I'd later face.

As I continue to walk in healing, wholeness, and purpose, I carry all of you with me. Your faith, your support, and your love are woven into every step. I hope this next chapter of my life, and this book, reflects not just my journey—but the power of legacy, grace, and redemption.

Thank you for being my foundation and my family. I love you deeply and honor your place in this journey.

With all my heart,

Leslie

A Letter to My Therapist

Dr. Reese,

There are no words that adequately capture the gratitude I feel for all you've done, but I'll try anyway—because you deserve that much and more.

Thank you for seeing me when I didn't know how to see myself and for hearing what I couldn't say out loud yet. Thank you for sitting with me in the darkest corners of my story without judgment, without rushing, and without fear. You've modeled what it means to hold sacred space for pain, process, and healing.

Week after week, you met me right where I was—whether I came in unraveling, armored up, or cautiously hopeful. You've been both an anchor and a compass, reminding me gently (and sometimes firmly!) that I don't have to carry what was never mine to begin with.

You taught me to be curious about my responses instead of condemning them. You challenged my patterns and invited me to notice. You reminded me that grace isn't just for the world—it's for me, too. With every word, every silence, every steady gaze, you helped me rebuild.

Because of you, I've learned to use my voice. To rest. To reframe. To grieve. To laugh. To believe that I am worthy of peace, not just survival. You've given me tools I'll carry for the rest of my life, and your presence in this chapter of my story is forever sacred.

Thank you for being a safe place, a wise guide, and a kind soul. Your work has changed my life—and I know I'm just one of many.

With honor and heartfelt gratitude,

Leslie

To My Circle – The Ones Who Stayed

There are no perfect words to fully express what you mean to me.
But this letter is my attempt to try.

To those of you who have stood in the trenches with me—not just
in the pretty moments, but in the messy, painful, raw seasons
where everything felt like it was falling apart—thank you. Truly.

You didn't flinch at the brokenness.
You didn't back away from the battles.
You didn't require performance or perfection.
Instead, you held space.
You offered prayers.
You lifted my arms when I didn't have the strength to lift them
myself.

There were times when I didn't even know what I needed... but you
showed up anyway.

You didn't need details to start interceding.
You didn't need explanations to believe in me.
You just kept showing up—with grace, with grit, and with
unwavering love.

You have been the hands and feet of Jesus in my life.
And I do not take that lightly.

This journey—this healing, this becoming—has not been easy. But
because of your presence, your steadiness, and your faith when
mine was weak, I never walked it alone.

You helped me remember who I was when I forgot.
You reminded me of what God said when the noise was too loud.

You reminded me I was never disqualified, even when shame tried to convince me otherwise.

Thank you for the texts that came right on time.
Thank you for the tears you've cried on my behalf.
Thank you for your fierce loyalty and gentle encouragement.

You've helped me come out of the fire not smelling like smoke.

This book, this season, this moment—it's as much yours as it is mine. Because healing happens in circles. Restoration happens in relationships. And God often sends His love through people like you.

You are my people.
You are my circle.
And I love you more than I can say.

Forever grateful,

Leslie

✦ 70 Biblical Truths to Replace the Lies We Tell Ourselves

Adapted from the book *Enough* by Sharon Jaynes

1. **Lie**: I'm not good enough.
   Truth: I am complete in Christ. *(Colossians 2:10)*
2. **Lie**: I'm unloved.
   Truth: I am deeply loved by God. *(Romans 5:5, John 3:16)*
3. **Lie**: I'll never be able to change.
   Truth: I am a new creation in Christ. *(2 Corinthians 5:17)*
4. **Lie**: I'm weak.
   Truth: I am strong in the Lord. *(Ephesians 6:10)*
5. **Lie**: I'm worthless.
   Truth: I am God's masterpiece. *(Ephesians 2:10)*
6. **Lie**: I'm all alone.
   Truth: God will never leave me. *(Hebrews 13:5)*
7. **Lie**: I've messed up too much.
   Truth: I am forgiven. *(1 John 1:9)*
8. **Lie**: I have no purpose.
   Truth: I was created for good works. *(Ephesians 2:10)*
9. **Lie**: I'm unwanted.
   Truth: I am chosen. *(1 Peter 2:9)*
10. **Lie**: God is mad at me.
    Truth: I am at peace with God. *(Romans 5:1)*
11. **Lie**: I can't hear God.
    Truth: I know His voice. *(John 10:27)*
12. **Lie**: My prayers don't matter.
    Truth: The prayers of the righteous are powerful. *(James 5:16)*
13. **Lie**: I'll never overcome this.
    Truth: I am more than a conqueror. *(Romans 8:37)*

14. **Lie**: I'm too broken.

    Truth: The Lord is close to the brokenhearted. *(Psalm 34:18)*
15. **Lie**: I'm too far gone.

    Truth: Nothing can separate me from God's love. *(Romans 8:38–39)*
16. **Lie**: I'm not strong enough.

    Truth: God's power is made perfect in my weakness. *(2 Corinthians 12:9)*
17. **Lie**: No one understands me.

    Truth: Jesus understands my every weakness. *(Hebrews 4:15)*
18. **Lie**: I'm not smart enough.

    Truth: I have the mind of Christ. *(1 Corinthians 2:16)*
19. **Lie**: I have no future.

    Truth: God has plans to give me hope. *(Jeremiah 29:11)*
20. **Lie**: I'm a failure.

    Truth: God works all things for my good. *(Romans 8:28)*
21. **Lie**: I don't fit in.

    Truth: I am a citizen of Heaven. *(Philippians 3:20)*
22. **Lie**: I'm not worth fighting for.

    Truth: God fights for me. *(Exodus 14:14)*
23. **Lie**: I can't do anything right.

    Truth: I can do all things through Christ. *(Philippians 4:13)*
24. **Lie**: I'm a victim.

    Truth: I have victory in Jesus. *(1 Corinthians 15:57)*
25. **Lie**: My body is broken.

    Truth: By His wounds, I am healed. *(Isaiah 53:5)*
26. **Lie**: I'm defined by my past.

    Truth: I am redeemed. *(Ephesians 1:7)*
27. **Lie**: I'm too anxious.

    Truth: God has not given me a spirit of fear. *(2 Timothy 1:7)*

28. **Lie**: I don't have what it takes.

   Truth: His divine power gives me everything I need. *(2 Peter 1:3)*

29. *Lie*: I'm too sinful.

   Truth: Where sin increased, grace increased more. *(Romans 5:20)*

30. **Lie**: No one sees me.

   Truth: God sees me and knows me. *(Genesis 16:13)*

31. **Lie**: I'm forgotten.

   Truth: God will never forget me. *(Isaiah 49:15)*

32. **Lie**: I'm a mistake.

   Truth: I am fearfully and wonderfully made. *(Psalm 139:14)*

33. **Lie**: I'm unqualified.

   Truth: God qualifies the called. *(2 Corinthians 3:5)*

34. **Lie**: My pain has no purpose.

   Truth: God uses everything for His glory. *(Romans 8:28)*

35. **Lie**: God doesn't care about the little things.

   Truth: He cares for me. *(1 Peter 5:7)*

36. **Lie**: I'm just too much.

   Truth: God delights in me. *(Zephaniah 3:17)*

37. **Lie**: I'll never be whole.

   Truth: God restores my soul. *(Psalm 23:3)*

38. **Lie**: I'm damaged goods.

   Truth: I am a vessel of honor. *(2 Timothy 2:21)*

39. **Lie**: My emotions make me weak.

   Truth: Jesus wept. *(John 11:35)*

40. **Lie**: I'll never change.

   Truth: God is doing a new thing in me. *(Isaiah 43:19)*

41. **Lie**: I'm stuck.

   Truth: God makes a way in the wilderness. *(Isaiah 43:19)*

42. **Lie**: I'm a burden.

   Truth: God carries me. *(Isaiah 46:4)*

43. **Lie**: I don't belong anywhere.

   Truth: I belong to Jesus. *(John 10:14)*

44. **Lie**: I can't get past this grief.

   Truth: God comforts those who mourn. *(Matthew 5:4)*

45. **Lie**: My story is too messy.

   Truth: God makes beauty from ashes. *(Isaiah 61:3)*

46. **Lie**: No one will ever accept me.

   Truth: I am accepted in the Beloved. *(Ephesians 1:6)*

47. **Lie**: My needs don't matter.

   Truth: God supplies all my needs. *(Philippians 4:19)*

48. **Lie**: God doesn't have time for me.

   Truth: God inclines His ear to me. *(Psalm 116:2)*

49. **Lie**: I've ruined everything.

   Truth: God restores the years the locust has eaten. *(Joel 2:25)*

50. **Lie**: I'll never be enough.

   Truth: God is my sufficiency. *(2 Corinthians 12:9)*

51. **Lie**: I can't do this anymore.

   Truth: God will renew my strength. *(Isaiah 40:31)*

52. **Lie**: I should give up.

   Truth: God rewards those who don't quit. *(Galatians 6:9)*

53. **Lie**: It's too late for me.

   Truth: God makes all things new. *(Revelation 21:5)*

54. **Lie**: I'll never be clean.

   Truth: I am washed by the Word. (Ephesians 5:26)

55. **Lie**: I don't matter.

   Truth: I am God's treasured possession. *(Deuteronomy 7:6)*

56. **Lie**: My thoughts will always torment me.

   Truth: I have the peace of God. *(Philippians 4:7)*

57. **Lie**: My life has no meaning.

   Truth: I was created with a purpose. *(Psalm 138:8)*

58. **Lie**: I'm not lovable.

   Truth: God's love is everlasting. *(Jeremiah 31:3)*

59. **Lie**: I'm invisible.

   Truth: God knows my name. *(Isaiah 43:1)*

60. **Lie**: I don't belong.

   Truth: I am part of God's family. *(Ephesians 2:19)*

61. **Lie**: I'm insignificant.

   Truth: I was knit together by God Himself. *(Psalm 139:13)*

62. **Lie**: I've wasted too much time.

   Truth: God restores. *(Joel 2:25)*

63. **Lie**: I'm too much for people.

   Truth: God knows me fully and still loves me. *(1 Corinthians 13:12)*

64. **Lie**: I've lost too much.

   Truth: God collects every tear. *(Psalm 56:8)*

65. **Lie**: I'm stuck in survival mode.

   Truth: Jesus came to give me abundant life. *(John 10:10)*

66. **Lie**: I've been rejected too often.

   Truth: God has accepted and adopted me. *(Romans 8:15)*

67. **Lie**: I'm not spiritual enough.

   Truth: God perfects me in His love. *(1 John 4:18)*

68. **Lie**: I'm not safe.

   Truth: God is my refuge and fortress. *(Psalm 91:2)*

69. **Lie**: I'll never be okay.

   Truth: God is working all things for good. *(Romans 8:28)*

70. **Lie**: I am what I've done.

   Truth: I am who God says I am. *(1 Peter 2:9)*

About the Author

Leslie Brennan
Speaker | Author | Coach | Realtor®
Founder of *Grace to Grow Circle* and *Leslie Brennan Speaks*

Your Next Chapter Starts Here.

If you've read this far, you know this isn't just a book—it's a breakthrough. Leslie Brennan has walked through shame, addiction, grief, healing, and grace, and she now uses her voice to help others find theirs. Whether you're looking for a speaker to inspire your event, a coach to walk alongside you, or resources to support your healing journey, Leslie offers wisdom from real-life experience wrapped in truth, Scripture, and fierce love.

🔲 Connect with Leslie Brennan

Want to learn more, book Leslie for a speaking event, or access powerful resources for healing and growth?

Ways to Connect:

🔲 Scan the QR code below to access Leslie's full link hub.

Email:

Leslie@lesliebrennanspeaks.com

Social:

✉ Leslie@LeslieBrennanSpeaks.com

▦ Instagram/Facebook: @LeslieBrennanSpeaks

Community:

Join the *Grace to Grow* Circle on Facebook

Real Estate:

Iron Valley Real Estate HR | www.targethomegroup.com

Looking for Hope? Hungry for Healing?

Reach out. You are not alone, and your story is not over.

Acknowledgments, Citations, and Resources

This book was written from the deepest places of my healing journey, and I owe much to the people, books, songs, scriptures, and professionals who helped guide me back to wholeness. The following sources have shaped, inspired, and supported the truths I've shared across these pages:

Scriptural References

All Scripture quotations are taken from the Holy Bible, New International Version® (NIV), unless otherwise noted.
Thank you to Bible Gateway for being a continual source of accessible truth throughout this journey.
Website: biblegateway.com

Professional & Clinical Inspiration

Dr. Kristin Neff – Self-Compassion
Website: self-compassion.org
Email: info@self-compassion.org

Dr. Brown – The Gifts of Imperfection, Shame and Vulnerability Research
Website: brenebrown.com

Melody Beattie – Codependent No More
Website: melodybeattie.com
Email: info@melodybeattie.com

Dr. Henry Cloud & Dr. John Townsend – Boundaries
Websites: drcloud.com and drtownsend.com

Dr. Claudia Black – Family Addiction Recovery & Generational Trauma Work
Website: claudiablack.com
Email: info@claudiablack.com

Steve Arterburn – Healing Is a Choice
Publisher: New Life Ministries
Website: newlife.com

🎵 Music That Spoke to My Soul

Megan Woods – The Truth
Songwriters: Jeff Pardo / Matthew West / Megan Woods
Lyrics used with permission, sourced from LyricFind
Publisher: Capitol CMG Publishing

💜 Devotional & Spiritual Encouragement

Mary Southerland – Devotions on Thought Life and God's Peace
Website: marysoutherland.com
Email: mary@marysoutherland.com

Mark Batterson – Win the Day
Publisher: Multnomah Books
Website: markbatterson.com

Dr. Ed Smith – Theophostic Prayer Ministry
Website: transformationprayer.org

Mental Health & Recovery Resources

Celebrate Recovery – Christ-Centered 12-Step Program
Website: celebraterecovery.com

Hope Christian Ministries – Christian Counseling & Family Support
Website: hcmva.com
Email: admin@hcmva.com

Travis Wallace & Sofia Perez – The FR4MULA
Support in food freedom, identity, and emotional health
Website: thefr4mula.com
Email: contact@thefr4mula.com

My Real-Life Teachers

To my therapist Dr. Reese, my children, my husband, my tribe, and my Savior—you have taught me what grace, healing, and daily freedom truly look like. Your fingerprints are all over these pages.